A Memoir
of
Robert Blincoe

by

John Brown

Manchester

1832

A MEMOIR
OF
ROBERT BLINCOE

An Orphan Boy;

SENT FROM THE WORKHOUSE OF ST. PANCRAS,
LONDON, AT SEVEN YEARS OF AGE,

TO ENDURE THE

Horrors of a Cotton-Mill,

THROUGH HIS INFANCY AND YOUTH,

WITH A MINUTE DETAIL OF HIS SUFFERINGS,

BEING THE FIRST MEMOIR OF THE KIND
PUBLISHED.

BY JOHN BROWN

MANCHESTER:
PRINTED FOR AND PUBLISHED
BY J. DOHERTY, 37 WITHY-GROVE

1832

CONTENTS

PUBLISHER'S PREFACE

The various Acts Of Parliament, which have been passed, to regulate the treatment of children in the Cotton Spinning Manufactories, betoken the previous existence of some treatment, so glaringly wrong, as to force itself upon the attention of the legislature. This Cotton-slave-trade, like the Negro-slave-trade, did not lack its defenders, and it might have afforded a sort of sorry consolation to the Negro slaves of America, had they been informed, that their condition, in having agriculturally to raise the cotton, was not half so bad, as that of the white infant-slaves, who had to assist in the spinning of it, when brought to this country. The religion and the black humanity of Mr. Wilberforce seem to have been entirely of a foreign nature. Pardon is begged, if an error is about to be wrongfully imputed—but the Publisher has no knowledge, that Mr. Wilberforce's humane advocacy for slaves, was ever of that homely kind, as to embrace the region of the home-cotton-slave-trade. And yet, who shall read the Memoir of Robert Blincoe, and say, that the charity towards slaves should not have begun or ended at home?

The Author of this Memoir is now dead; he fell, about two or three years ago, by his own hand. He united, with a strong feeling for the injuries and sufferings of others, a high sense of injury when it bore on himself, whether real or imaginary; and a despondency when his prospects were not good.—Hence his suicide.—Had he not possessed a fine fellow-feeling with the child of misfortune, he had never taken such pains to compile the[iv] Memoir of Robert Blincoe, and to collect all the wrongs on paper, on which he could gain information, about the various sufferers under the cotton-mill systems. Notes to the Memoir of Robert Blincoe were intended by the author, in illustration of his strong personal assertions. The references were marked in the Memoir; but the Notes were not prepared, or if prepared, have not come to the Publisher's hand. But, on inquiring after Robert Blincoe, in Manchester, and mentioning the Memoir of him written by Mr. Brown, as being in the Publisher's possession, other papers, by the same Author, which had been left on a loan of money in Manchester, were obtained, and these papers seem to have formed the authorities, from which the Notes to the Memoirs would have been made. So that, though the Publisher does not presume to make notes for the Author, nor for himself, to this Memoir, he is prepared to confirm much of the statement here made, the personalities of Robert Blincoe excepted, should it be generally challenged.

Robert Blincoe, the subject of the Memoir, is now about 35 years of age, and resides at No. 19, Turner-street, Manchester, where he keeps a small grocer's shop. He is also engaged in manufacturing Sheet Wadding and Cotton Waste-Dealer. The Publisher having no knowledge of Robert Blincoe, but in common with every reader of this Memoir, can have no personal feelings towards him, other than those of pity for his past sufferings. But such a Memoir as this was much wanted, to hand down to posterity, what was the real character of the complaints about the treatment of children in our cotton mills, about which a legislation has taken place, and so much has been said. An amended treatment of children has been made, the apprenticing system having been abandoned by the masters of the mills; but the employment is in itself bad for children—first, as their health—and second, as to their manners and acquirements—the employment being in a bad atmosphere; and the education, from example, being bad; the time that should be[v] devoted to a better education, being devoted to that which is bad. The employment of infant children in the cotton-mills furnishes a bad means to dissolute parents, to live in idleness and all sorts of vice, upon the produce of infant labour. There is much of this in Lancashire, which a little care and looking after, on the part of the masters of cotton-mills, might easily prevent. But what is to be done? Most of the extensive manufacturers profit by human misery and become callous toward it; both from habit and interest. If a remedy be desired, it must be sought by that part of the working people themselves, who are alive to their progressing degradation. It will never be sought fairly out, by those who have no interest in seeking it. And so long as the majority of the working people squanders its already scanty income in those pest-houses, those intoxicating nurseries, for vice, idleness and misery, the public drinking-houses, there is no hope for them of an amended condition.

---

*This publisher's preface was included in the original 1832 publication.

CHAPTER I.

By the time the observant reader has got through the melancholy recital of the sufferings of Blincoe and his associates in cotton-mill bondage, he will probably incline to an opinion, that rather than rear destitute and deserted children, to be thus distorted by excessive toil, and famished and tortured as those have been, it were incomparably less cruel to put them at once to death—less cruel that they had never been born alive; and far more wise that they had never been conceived. In cases of unauthorized pregnancies, our laws are tender of unconscious life, perhaps to a faulty extreme; whilst our parochial institutions, as these pages will prove, after incurring considerable expence to PRESERVE the lives of those forlorn beings, sweep them off by shoals, under the sanction of other legal enactments, and consign them to a fate, far worse than sudden death.

Reared in the most profound ignorance and depravity, these unhappy beings are, from the hour of their birth, to the last of their existence, generally cut off from all that is decent in social life. Their preceptors are the veriest wretches in nature!—their influential examples all of the worst possible kind. The reports of the Cotton Bill Committees abundantly prove, that, by forcing those destitute poor to go into cotton-mills, they have, in very numerous instances, been consigned to a destiny worse than death without torture. Yet appalling as are many of the statements, which, through the reports of the Committees, have found their way before the public, similar acts of delinquencies, of a hue still

1

darker—even repeated acts of murder, have escaped unnoticed. Much of the evidence brought forward by the friends of humanity, was neutralized or frittered away by timidity of their witnesses, or by the base subserviency of venally unprincipled professional men, who, influenced by rich capitalists, basely prostituted their talent and character as physicians, surgeons, and apothecaries, to deceive the government, to perplex and mislead public opinion, and avert the loud cry raised against the insatiate avarice and relentless cruelty of their greedy and unfeeling suborners.

It was in the spring of 1822, after having devoted a considerable time to the investigating of the effect of the manufacturing system, and factory establishments, on the health and morals of the manufacturing populace, that I first heard of the extraordinary sufferings of R. Blincoe. At the same time, I was told of his earnest wish that those sufferings should, for the protection of the rising generation of parish children, be laid before the world. Thus assured, I went to enquire for him, and was much pleased with his conversation. If this young man had not been consigned to a cotton-factory, he would probably have been strong, healthy, and well grown; instead of which, he is diminutive as to stature, and his knees are grievously distorted. In his manners, he appeared remarkably gentle; in his language, temperate; in his statements, cautious and consistent. If, in any part of the ensuing narrative, there are falsehoods and misrepresentations, the fault rests solely with himself; for, repeatedly and earnestly, I admonished him to beware, lest a too keen remembrance of the injustice he had suffered should lead him to transgress the limits of truth. After I had taken down his communications, I tested them, by reading the same to other persons, with whom Blincoe had not had any intercourse on the subject, and who had partaken of the miseries of the same hard servitude, and by whom they were in every point confirmed.

ROBERT BLINCOE commenced his melancholy narrative, by stating, that he was a parish orphan, and knew not either his father or mother. From the age of four years, he says, "till I had completed my seventh, I was supported in Saint Pancras poorhouse, near London." In very pathetic terms, he frequently censured and regretted the remissness of the parish officers, who, when they

2

received him into the workhouse, had, as he seemed to believe, neglected to make any entry, or, at least, any to which he could obtain access, of his mother's and father's name, occupation, age, or residence. Blincoe argued, and plausibly too, that those officers would not have received him, if his mother had not proved her settlement; and he considered it inhuman in the extreme, either to neglect to record the names of his parents, or, if recorded, to refuse to give him that information, which, after his attaining his freedom, he had requested at their hands. His lamentations, on this head, were truely touching, and evinced a far higher degree of susceptibility of heart, than could have been expected from the extreme and long continued wretchedness he had endured in the den of vice and misery, where he was so long immured. Experience often evinces, that, whilst moderate adversity mollifies and expands the human heart, extreme and long continued wretchedness has a direct and powerful contrary tendency, and renders it impenetrably callous.

In one of our early interviews, tears trickling down his pallid cheeks, and his voice tremulous and faltering, Blincoe said, "I am worse off than a child reared in the Foundling Hospital. Those orphans have a name given them by the heads of that institution, at the time of baptism, to which they are legally entitled. But I have no name I can call my own." He said he perfectly recollected riding in a coach to the workhouse, accompanied by some female, that he did not however think this female was his mother, for he had not the least consciousness of having felt either sorrow or uneasiness at being separated from her, as he very naturally supposed he should have felt, if that person had been his mother. Blincoe also appeared to think he had not been nursed by his mother, but had passed through many hands before he arrived at the workhouse; because he had no recollection of ever having experienced a mother's caresses. It seems, young as he was, he often enquired of the nurses, when the parents and relations of other children came to see his young associates, *why no one came to him*, and used to weep, when he was told, that *no one had ever owned him*, after his being placed in that house. Some of the nurses stated, that a female, who called soon after his arrival, inquired for him by the name of "Saint;" and, when he was produced, gave him a penny-piece, and told him his mother was dead. If this report were well founded, his mother's illness was the cause of his being removed and sent to the workhouse. According to his own description, he felt with extreme sensibility the loneliness of his condition, and, at each stage of his future sufferings, during his severe cotton-mill servitude, it pressed on his heart the heaviest of all his sorrows—an impassable barrier, "a wall of brass," cut him off from all mankind. The sad consciousness, that he stood alone *"a waif on the world's wide common;"* that he had no acknowledged claim of kindred with any human being, rich or poor—that he stood apparently for ever excluded from every social circle, so constantly occupied his thoughts, that, together with his sufferings, they imprinted a pensive character on his features, which probably neither change of fortune, nor time itself, would ever entirely obliterate. When he was six years old, and, as the workhouse children were saying their Catechism, it was his turn to repeat the Fifth Commandment—"Honour thy father and thy mother, &c.," he recollects having suddenly burst into tears, and felt greatly agitated and distressed—his voice faltering, and his limbs trembling. According to his statement, and his pathetic eloquence, in reciting his misfortunes, strongly corroborated his assertion, he was a very ready scholar, and the source of this sudden burst of grief being inquired into by some of his superiors, he said, "I cry, because *I cannot* obey one of God's commandments, I know not either my father or my mother, I cannot therefore be a good child and honour my parents."

It was rumoured, in the ward where Robert Blincoe was placed, that he owed his existence to the mutual frailties of his mother and a reverend divine, and was called the young Saint, in allusion to his priestly descent. This name or appellation he did not long retain, for he was afterwards called Parson; often, *the young Parson*; and he recollected hearing it said in his presence, that he was the son of a parson Blincoe. Whether these allusions were founded in truth, or were but the vile effusions of vulgar malice, was not, and is not, in his power to determine, whose bosom they have so painfully agitated. Another remarkable circumstance in his case, was, that when he was sent in August, 1799, with a large number of other children, from Saint Pancras workhouse, to a cotton-mill near Nottingham, he bore amongst his comrades, the name of *Parson*, and retained it afterwards till he had served considerably longer than his FOURTEEN YEARS, and then, when his Indentures were at last relinquished, and not till then, the young man found he had been apprenticed by the name of Robert Blincoe. I urged the probability, that his right indenture might, in the change of masters that took place, or the careless indifference of his last master, have been given to another boy, and that to the one given to him, bearing the name of Blincoe, he had no just claim. This reasoning he repelled, by steadily and consistently asserting, he fully recollected having heard it said his real name was Blincoe, whilst he remained at Saint Pancras workhouse. His indentures were dated the 15th August, 1799. If, at this time, he was seven years of age, which is by no means certain, he was born in 1792, and in 1796, was placed in Pancras workhouse. With these remarks I close this preliminary matter, and happy should I be, if the publication of these facts enables the individual to whom they relate, to remove the veil which has hitherto deprived him of a knowledge of his parentage, a privation which he still appears to feel with undiminished intensity of grief.

Two years have elapsed, since I first began to take notes of Blincoe's extraordinary narrative. At the close of 1822 and beginning of 1823, I was seized with a serious illness, which wholly prevented my publishing this and other important communications. The testimony of a respectable surgeon, who attended me, as any in the country, even ocular demonstration of my enfeebled state, failed to convince some of the cotton spinners, that my inability was not feigned, to answer some sinister end; and such atrocious conduct was pursued towards me, as would have fully justified a prosecution for conspiracy. Animated by the most opposite views, the worst of miscreants united to vilify and oppress me; the one wanting to get my papers, in order, by destroying them, to prevent the enormities of the cotton masters being exposed; and another, traducing my character, and menacing my life, under an impression that I had basely sold the declarations and communications received from oppressed work-people to their masters. By some of those suspicious, misjudging people, Blincoe was led away. He did not, however, at any time, or under any circumstances, retract or deny any part of his communications, and, on the 18th and 19th of March, 1824, of his own free will, he not only confirmed all that he had communicated in the spring of 1822, with many other traits of suffering, not then recollected, but furnished me with them. It has, therefore, stood the test of this hurricane, without its authenticity being in any one part questioned or impaired. The authenticity of this narrative is, therefore, entitled to greater credit, than much of the testimony given by the owners of cotton-factories, or by professional men on their behalf, as will, in the course of this narrative, be fully demonstrated, by evidence wholly incontrovertible. If, therefore, it should be proved, that atrocities to the same extent, exist no longer; still, its publication, as a preventative remedy, is no less essential to the protection of parish paupers and foundlings. If the gentlemen of Manchester and its vicinity, who acted in 1816, &c., in conjunction with the late Mr. Nathaniel Gould, had not made the selection of witnesses too much in the power of incompetent persons, Robert Blincoe would have been selected in 1819, as the most impressive pleader in behalf of destitute and deserted children.

CHAPTER II.

Of the few adventures of Robert Blincoe, during his residence in old Saint Pancras workhouse, the principal occurred when he had been there about two years. He acknowledges he was well fed, decently clad, and comfortably lodged, and not at all overdone, as regarded work; yet, with all these blessings in possession, this destitute child grew melancholy. He relished none of the humble comforts he enjoyed. It was liberty he wanted. The busy world lay outside the workhouse gates, and those he was seldom, if ever permitted to pass. He was cooped up in a gloomy, though liberal sort of a prison-house. His buoyant spirits longed to rove at large. He was too young to understand the necessity of the restraint to which he was subjected, and too opinionative to admit it could be intended for his good. Of the world he knew nothing, and the society of a workhouse was not very well calculated to delight the mind of a volatile child. He saw givers, destitute of charity, receivers of insult, instead of gratitude, witnessed little besides sullenness and discontent, and heard little but murmurs or malicious and slanderous whispers. The aged were commonly petulant and miserable—the young demoralized and wholly destitute of gaiety of heart. From the top to the bottom, the whole of this motley mass was tainted with dissimulation, and he saw the most abhorrent hypocrisy in constant operation. Like a bird newly caged, that flutters from side to side, and foolishly beats its wings against its prison walls, in hope of obtaining its liberty, so young Blincoe, weary of confinement and resolved, if possible to be free, often watched the outer gates of the house, in the hope, that some favourable opportunity might facilitate his escape. He wistfully measured the height of the wall, and found it too lofty for him to scale, and too well guarded were the gates to admit of his egress unnoticed. His spirits, he says, which were naturally lively and buoyant, sank under this vehement longing after liberty. His appetite declined, and he wholly forsook his usual sports and comrades. It is hard to say how this disease of the mind might have terminated, if an accident had not occurred, which afforded a chance of emerging from the lifeless monotony of a workhouse, and of launching into the busy world, with which he longed to mingle.

Blincoe declares, he was so weary of confinement, he would gladly have exchanged situations with the poorest of the poor children, whom, from the upper windows of the workhouse, he had seen begging from door to door, or, as a subterfuge, offering matches for sale. Even the melancholy note of the sweep-boy, whom, long before day, and in the depths of winter, in frost, in snow, in rain, in sleet, he heard pacing behind his surly master, had no terrors for him. So far from it, he envied him his fortune, and, in the fulness of discontent, thought his own state incomparably more wretched. The poor child was suffering under a diseased imagination, from which men of mature years and elaborate culture are not always free. It filled his heart with perverted feelings—it rendered the little urchin morose and unthankful, and, as undeserving of as he was insensible to, the important benefits extended to him by a humane institution, when helpless, destitute and forlorn.

From this state of early misanthropy, young Blincoe was suddenly diverted, by a rumour, that filled many a heart among his comrades with terror, viz. that a day was appointed, when the master-sweeps of the metropolis were to come and select such a number of boys as apprentices, till they attained the age of 21 years, as they might deign to take into their sable fraternity. These tidings, that struck damp to the heart of the other boys, sounded like heavenly music to the ears of young Blincoe:—he anxiously inquired of the nurses if the news were true, and if so, what chance there was of his being one of the elect. The ancient matrons, amazed at the boy's temerity and folly, told him how bitterly he would rue the day that should consign him to that wretched employment, and bade him pray earnestly to God to protect him from such a destiny. The young adventurer heard these opinions with silent contempt. Finding, on farther inquiry, that the rumour was well founded, he applied to several menials in the house, whom he thought likely to promote his suit, entreating them to forward his election with all the interest they could command! Although at this time he was a fine grown boy, being fearful he might be deemed too low in stature, he accustomed himself to walk in an erect posture, and went almost a tip-toe;—by a ludicrous conceit, he used to hang by the hands to the rafters and balustrades, supposing that an exercise, which could only lengthen his arms, would produce the same effect on his legs and body. In this course of training for the contingent honour of being chosen by the master-sweeps, as one fit for their use,—with a perseverance truly admirable, his tender age considered, young Blincoe continued till the important day arrived. The boys were brought forth, many of them in tears, and all except Blincoe, very sorrowful. Amongst them, by an act unauthorised by his guardians, young Blincoe contrived to intrude his person. His deportment formed a striking contrast to that of all his comrades; his seemed unusually high: he smiled as the grim looking fellows approached him; held his head as high as he could, and, by every little artifice in his power, strove to attract their notice, and obtain the honour of their preference. While this fatherless and motherless child, with an intrepid step, and firm countenance, thus courted the smiles of the sooty tribe, the rest of the boys conducted themselves as if they nothing so much dreaded, as to become the objects of their choice, and shrunk back from their touch as if they had been tainted by the most deadly contagion. Boy after boy was taken, in preference to Blincoe, who was often handled, examined, and rejected. At the close of the show, the number required was elected, and Blincoe was not among them! He declared, that his chagrin was inexpressible, when his failure was apparent.

Some of the sweeps complimented him for his spirit, and, to console him, said, if he made a good use of his time, and contrived to grow a head taller, he might do very well for a fag, at the end of a couple of years. This disappointment gave a severe blow to the aspiring ambition of young Blincoe, whose love of liberty was so ardent, that he cared little about the sufferings by which, if attained, it was likely to be alloyed. The boys that were chosen, were not immediately taken away. Mingling with these, some of them said to our hero, the tears standing in their eyes:—"why, Parson, can you endure the thoughts of going to be a chimney-sweep? I wish they would take you instead of me." "So do I, with all my heart," said Blincoe, "for I would rather be any where than here." At night, as Blincoe lay tossing about, unable to sleep, because he had been rejected, his unhappy associates were weeping and wailing, because they had been accepted! Yet, his heart was not so cold as to be unaffected by the wailings of those poor children, who, mournfully anticipating the horrors of their new calling, deplored their misfortune in the most touching terms. They called upon their parents, who, living or dead, were alike unable to hear them, to come and save them! What a difference of feeling amongst children of the same unfortunate class! The confinement that was so wearisome to young Blincoe, must have been equally irksome to some of his young associates; therefore, the love of liberty could not have been its sole cause,—there was another and a stronger reason—all his comrades had friends, parents, or relations: poor Blincoe stood alone! no ties of consanguinity or kindred bound him to any particular portion of society, or to any place—he had no friend to soothe his troubled mind—no domestic circle to which, though excluded for a time, he might hope to be reunited. As he stood thus estranged from the common ties of nature, it is the less to be wondered at, that, propelled by a violent inclination to a rambling life, and loathing the restraint imposed by his then condition, he should indulge so preposterous a notion, as to prefer the wretched state of a sweeping-boy. Speaking on this subject, Blincoe said to me, "If I could penetrate the source of my exemption from the sorrow and consternation so forcibly expressed by my companions, it would probably have been resolved by the peculiarity of my destiny, and the privation of those endearing ties and ligatures which cement family circles. When the friends, relatives, parents of other children came to visit them, the caresses that were sometimes exchanged, the joy that beamed on the faces of those so favoured, went as daggers to my heart; not that I cherished a feeling of envy at their good fortune; but that it taught me more keenly to feel my own forlorn condition. Sensations, thus, excited, clouded every festive hour, and, young as I was, the voice of nature, instinct, if you will, forced me to consider myself as a moral outcast, as a scathed and blighted tree, in the midst of a verdant lawn."

I dare not aver, that such were the very words Blincoe used, but they faithfully convey the spirit and tendency of his language and sentiments. Blincoe is by no means deficient in understanding: he can be witty, satirical, and pathetic, by turns, and he never showed himself to such advantage, as when expatiating upon the desolate state to which his utter ignorance of his parentage had reduced him.

During Blincoe's abode at St. Pancras, he was inoculated at the Small Pox Hospital. He retained a vivid remembrance of the copious doses of salts he had to swallow, and that his heart heaved, and his hand shook as the nauseous potion approached his lips. The old nurse seemed to consider such conduct as being wholly unbecoming a *pauper child*; and chiding young Blincoe, told him, he ought to "lick his lips," and say thank you, for the good and wholesome medicine provided for him at the public expense; at the same time, very coarsely reminding him of the care that was taken to save him from an untimely death by catching the small-pox in the natural way. In the midst of his subsequent afflictions, in Litton Mill, Blincoe, declared, he often lamented having, by this inoculation, lost a chance of escaping by an early death, the horrible destiny for which he was preserved.

From the period of Blincoe's disappointment, in being rejected by the sweeps, a sudden calm seems to have succeeded, which lasted till a rumour ran through the house, that a treaty was on foot between the Churchwardens and Overseers of St. Pancras, and the owner of a great cotton factory, in the vicinity of Nottingham, for the disposal of a large number of children, as apprentices, till they become twenty-one years of age. This occurred about a twelvemonth after his chimney-sweep miscarriage. The rumour itself inspired Blincoe with new life and spirits; he was in a manner intoxicated with joy, when he found, it was not only confirmed, but that the number required was so considerable, that it would take off the greater part of the children in the house,—poor infatuated boy! delighted with the hope of obtaining a greater degree of liberty than he was allowed in the workhouse,—he dreamed not of the misery that impended, in the midst of which he could look back to Pancras as to an Elysium, and bitterly reproach himself for his ingratitude and folly.

Prior to the show-day of the pauper children to the purveyor or cotton master, the most illusive and artfully contrived falsehoods were spread, to fill the minds of those poor infants with the most absurd and ridiculous errors, as to the real nature of the servitude, to which they were to be consigned. It was gravely stated to them, according to Blincoe's statement, made in the most positive and solemn manner, that they were all, when they arrived at the cotton-mill, to be transformed into ladies and gentlemen: that they would be fed on roast beef and plum-pudding—be allowed to ride their masters' horses, and have silver watches, and plenty of cash in their pockets. Nor was it the nurses, or other inferior persons of the workhouse, with whom this vile deception originated; but with the parish officers themselves. From the statement of the victims of cotton-mill bondage, it seems to have been a constant rule, with those who had the disposal of parish children, prior to sending them off to cotton-mills, to fill their minds with the same delusion. Their hopes being thus excited, and their imaginations inflamed, it was next stated, amongst the innocent victims of fraud and deception, that no one could be *compelled* to go, nor any but volunteers accepted.

When it was supposed at St. Pancras, that these excitements had operated sufficiently powerful to induce a ready acquiescence in the proposed migration, all the children, male and female, who were seven years old, or considered to be of that age, were assembled in the committee-room, for the purpose of being publicly examined, touching their health, and capacity, and what is almost incredible touching their *willingness* to go and serve as apprentices, in the way and manner required! There is something so detestable, in this proceeding, that any one might conclude, that Blincoe had been misled in his recollections of the particulars; but so many other sufferers have corroborated his statement, that I can entertain no doubt of the fact. This exhibition took place in August

1799, and eighty boys and girls as parish apprentices, and till they had respectively acquired the age of twenty-one years, were made over by the churchwardens and overseers of Saint Pancras parish, to Messrs. Lamberts', cotton-spinners, hosiers and lace-men, of St. Mary's parish, Nottingham, the owners of Lowdam Mill. The boys, during the latter part of their time, were to be instructed in the trade of stocking weaving—the girls in lace-making. There was no specification whatever, as to the time their masters were to be allowed to work these poor children, although, at this period, the most abhorrent cruelties were notoriously known to be exercised, by the owners of cotton-mills, upon parish apprentices. According to Blincoe's testimony, so powerfully had the illusions, purposely spread to entrap these poor children, operated, and so completely were their feeble minds excited, by the blandishments held out to them, that they almost lost their wits. They thought and talked of nothing but the scenes of luxury and grandeur, in which they were to move. Nor will the reflecting reader feel surprised at this credulity, however gross, when he considers the poor infants imagined there were no greater personages than the superiors, to whom they were, as paupers, subjected, and that, it was those identical persons, by whom their weak and feeble intellects had thus been imposed upon. Blincoe describes his conduct to have been marked by peculiar extravagance. Such was his impatience, he could scarcely eat or sleep, so anxiously did he wait the hour of emancipation. The poor deluded young creatures were so inflated with pride and vanity, that they strutted about like so many dwarfish and silly kings and queens, in a mock tragedy. "We began" said Blincoe "to treat our old nurses with airs of insolence and disdain—refused to associate with children, who, from sickness, or being under age, had not been accepted; they were commanded to keep their distance; told to know their betters; forbidden to mingle in our exalted circle! Our little coterie was a complete epitome of the effects of prosperity in the great world. No sooner were our hearts cheered by a prospect of good fortune, than its influence produced the sad effects recited. The germ of those hateful vices, arrogance, selfishness and ingratitude, began to display themselves even before we had tasted the intoxicating cup. But our illusion soon vanished, and we were suddenly awakened from the flattering dream, which consigned the greater part of us to a fate more severe than that of the West Indian slaves, who have the good fortune to serve humane owners." Such were Blincoe's reflections in May 1822.

It appears that the interval was not long, which filled up the space between their examination, acceptance, and departure from St. Pancras workhouse, upon their way to Nottingham; but short as it was, it left room for dissension. The boys could not agree who should have the *first ride* on their masters' horses, and violent disputes arose amongst the girls, on subjects equally ludicrous. It was afterwards whispered at Lowdam Mill, that the elder girls, previous to leaving Pancras, began to feel scruples, whether their dignity would allow them to drop the usual bob-curtsey to the master or matron of the house, or to the governess by whom they had been instructed to read, or work by the needle. Supposing all these follies to have been displayed to the very letter, the poor children were still objects of pity; the guilt rests upon those by whom they had been so wickedly deceived!

Happy, no doubt, in the thought of transferring the burthen of the future support of fourscore young paupers to other parishes, the churchwardens and overseers distinguished the departure of this juvenile colony by acts of munificence. The children were completely new clothed, and each had two suits, one for their working, the other for their holiday dress—a shilling in money, was given to each—a new pocket handkerchief—and a large piece of gingerbread. As Blincoe had no relative of whom to take leave, all his anxiety was to get outside the door. According to his own account, he was the first at the gate, one of the foremost who mounted the waggon, and the loudest in his cheering. In how far the parents or relatives of the rest of the children consented to this migration; if they were at all consulted, or even apprised of its being in contemplation, formed no part of Blincoe's communications. All he stated was, that the whole of the party seemed to start in very high spirits. As to his own personal conduct, Blincoe asserts, he strutted along dressed in party-coloured parish clothing, on his way to the waggon, no less filled with vanity than with delusion: he imagined he was free, when he was in fact legally converted into a slave; he exulted in the imaginary possession of personal liberty, when he was in reality a prisoner. The whole convoy were well guarded by the parish beadles on their way to the waggons; but those officers, bearing their staves, the children were taught to consider as a guard of *honour*. In addition to the beadles, there was an active young man or two, appointed to look after the passengers of the two large waggons, in their conveyance to Nottingham. Those vehicles, and very properly too, were so secured, that when once the grated doors were locked, no one could escape. Plenty of clean straw was strewed in the beds, and no sooner were the young fry *safely lodged* within, than they began throwing it over one another and seemed delighted with the commencement of their journey. A few hours progress considerably damped this exultation. The inequality of the road, and the heavy jolts of the waggon, occasioned them many a bruise. Although it was the middle of August, the children felt very uncomfortable. The motion of the heavy clumsey vehicle, and so many children cooped up in so small a space, produced nausea and other results, such as sometimes occur in Margate boys. Of the country they passed through, the young travellers saw very little.— Blincoe thinks the children were suffered to come out of the waggon to walk through St. Alban's. After having passed one night in the waggon, many of the children began to repent, and express a wish to return. They were told to have patience, till they arrived at Messrs. Lamberts, when, *no doubt*, those gentlemen would pay every attention to their wishes, and send back to St. Pancras, those who might wish to return. Blincoe, as might have been expected, was not one of those *back-sliders*—he remained steady to his purpose, exulting in the thought, that every step he advanced brought him nearer to the desired spot, where so many enviable enjoyments awaited him, and conveyed him farther and farther from the detested workhouse! Blincoe being so overjoyed with the fine expectations he was to receive at Lowdam Mill, he spent his shilling at Leicester in apples.

The greater part of the children were much exhausted, and not a few of them seriously indisposed, before they arrived at Nottingham. When the waggons drew up near the dwelling and warehouse of their future master, a crowd collected to see the *live stock* that was just imported from the metropolis, who were pitied, admired, and compared to lambs, led by butchers to slaughter! Care was taken that they should not hear or understand much of this sort of discourse. The boys and girls were distributed, some in the kitchen, others in a large ware-room, washed, combed and supplied with refreshments; but there were no plum-pudding—no roast beef, no talk of the horses they were to ride, nor of the watches and fine clothing that they had been promised. Many looked very mournful; they had been four days travelling to Nottingham: at a more advanced period of their lives, a travel to the East Indies might not have been estimated as a much more important or hazardous undertaking. After having been well refreshed, the whole of the boys and girls were drawn up in rows, to be *reviewed by their masters*, their friends and neighbours. In Blincoe's estimation, their masters, Messrs. Lamberts', were "stately sort of men." They looked over the children and finding them all right, according to the INVOICE, exhorted them to behave with proper humility and decorum. To pay the most prompt and submissive respects to the orders of those who would be appointed to instruct and superintend them at Lowdam Mill, and to be diligent and careful, each one to execute his or her task, and thereby avoid the punishment and disgrace which awaited idleness, insolence, or disobedience. This harangue, which was delivered in a severe and dictatorial tone, increased their apprehensions, but not one durst open a mouth to complain. The masters and their servants talked of the various sorts of labour to which the children were to apply themselves, and to the consternation and dismay of Blincoe and his associates, not the least allusion was made to the many fine things which had so positively been promised them whilst in London. The conversation which Blincoe heard, seemed to look forward to close, if not to unremitting toil, and the poor boy had been filled with expectations, that he was to work only when it pleased him; to have abundance of money and fine clothes—a watch in his pocket, to feast on roast beef and plum-pudding, and to ride his masters horses. His hopes, however were, not wholly extinguished, because Nottingham was not Lowdam Mill, but his confidence was greatly reduced, and his tone of exultation much lowered.

The children rested one night at Nottingham in the warehouses of their new masters—the next day they were led out to see the castle, Mortimer-hole and other local curiosities, in the forest of Sherwood, which are so celebrated by bards of ancient times. Many shoes, bonnets, and many other articles of clothing having been lost upon the journey, others were supplied—but withal Blincoe found himself treated as a parish orphan, and he calculated on being received and treated as if he had been a gentleman's son sent on a visit to the house of a friend or relative. By the concurring testimony of other persons who had been entrapped by similar artifices, it appears certain, that the *purveyors* of infant labourers to supply the masters of cotton and silk factories with cheap labourers, adopted this vile, unmanly expedient, in most of their transactions. It will be seen, by the evidence of Sir Robert Peel, Baronet, David Owen, Esq. and other witnesses examined in 1816, that, when children were first wanted to attend machinery in cotton-factories, such was the aversion of parents and guardians to this noxious employment, that scarcely any would submit to consign their offspring to those mills, the owners of which, under the specious pretext of diminishing the burdens occasioned by poor-rates, prevailed on churchwardens and overseers, to put their infant paupers into their hands. Since then, by a gradual progress of poverty and depravity, in the county of Lancashire alone, there are some thousand fathers, mothers, and relatives, who live upon the produce of infant labour, though alloyed by the dreadful certainty, that their gain is acquired by the sacrifice of their children's health and morals, and too frequently of their lives, whereby the fable of Saturn devouring his children, seems realised in modern times.

CHAPTER III.

Lowdham Cotton-Mill, situated near a village of that name, stood ten miles distant from Nottingham, on the Surhill road; thither Robert Blincoe and his associates were conveyed the next day in carts, and it was rather late when they arrived. The mill, a large and lofty edifice, being surmounted by a cupola, Blincoe, at first, mistook for a church, which raised a laugh at his expense, and some jeering remarks, that he would soon know what sort of service was performed there. Another said, he did not doubt but the young cocknies would be very *regular* in their *attendance*. When he came in view of the apprentice-house, which was half a mile distant from the mill, and was told that was *to be his home for fourteen years to come*, he was not greatly delighted, so closely did it resemble a workhouse. There was one source of consolation, however, remaining—it was not surrounded by lofty walls, nor secured by strong gates, as was the case at Pancras. When the first cart, in which was young Blincoe, drove up to the door, a number of villagers flocked round, some of whom exclaimed, "God help the poor wretches."—"Eh!" said another, "what a fine collection of children, little do they know to what a life of slavery they are doomed."—"The Lord have mercy upon them," said a third.— "They'll find little mercy here," said a fourth. The speakers were mostly of the female sex, who, shaking their heads, said,—"Ah! what fine clear complexions!"—"The roses will soon be out of bloom in the mill." Such were a part of the remarks which saluted the ears of these children, as they entered the Lowdham Mill. In common with his comrades, Blincoe was greatly dismayed, by the

18

gloomy prognostications, which their guardians did all they could to check, or prevent the children from hearing, hurrying them, as rapidly as they could, inside the house.

The young strangers were conducted into a spacious room, fitted up in the style of the dinner-room, in Pancras old workhouse, viz: with long, narrow deal tables, and wooden benches. Although the rooms seemed tolerably clean, there was a certain rank, oily, smell, which Blincoe did not very much admire. They were ordered to sit down at these tables—the boys and girls apart. The other apprentices had not left work, when this supply of children arrived. The supper set before them consisted of milk-porridge, of a very blue complexion! The bread was partly made of rye—very black, and so soft, they could scarcely swallow it, as it stuck like bird-lime to their teeth. Poor Blincoe stared, recollecting this was not so good a fare as they had been used to at Saint Pancras. Where is our roast beef and plum-pudding, he said to himself. He contrived, with some difficulty, to eat about one half of his allowance. As the young strangers gazed mournfully at each other, the governor and governess, as the master and mistress of the apprentices were styled, kept walking round them, and making very coarse remarks. Just as they had passed Blincoe, some of the girls began making faces, and one flung a dab of bread against the wall, where it stuck fast, as if it had been plaister. This caught the eye of the governor—a huge raw-boned man, who had served in the army, and had been a drill serjeant, unexpectedly, he produced a large horse-whip, which he clanged in such a sonorous manner, that it made the house re-echo. In a moment, the face-makers and bread throwers were reduced to solemn silence and abject submission. Even young Blincoe was daunted—he had been one of the ring-leaders in these seditious proceedings; but so powerful was the shock to his nerves, sustained from the tremendous clang of the horse-whip, it bereft him of all his gaity, and he sat as demure as a truant-scholar, just previous to his flogging. Yet the master of the house had not uttered a single threat; nor indeed had he occasion; his carbuncled nose—his stern and forbidding aspect and his terrible horse-whip, inspired quite as much terror as was requisite. Knowing that the apprentices from the mill were coming, this formidable being retired, to the great relief of the young strangers, but so deep an impression had he created, they sat erect and formal, scarcely daring to look beyond the nose. Whilst they were in this subdued and neutralised state, their attention was suddenly and powerfully attracted by the loud shouting of many voices, almost instantly the stone-room filled, spacious as it was, with a multitude of young persons of both sexes; from young women down to mere children. Their presence was accompanied by a scent of no very agreeable nature, arising from the grease and dirt acquired in the avocation.

The boys, generally speaking, had nothing on, but a shirt and trousers. Some few, and but a few, had jackets and hats. Their coarse shirts were entirely open at the neck, and their hair looked, as if a comb had seldom, if ever, been applied! The girls, as well as Blincoe could recollect, were, like the boys, destitute of shoes and stockings. Their locks were pinned up, and they were without caps; very few had on, either jacket or gown; but wore, what, in London, are called pinafores; in Lancashire, bishops!—that is, long aprons with sleeves, made of coarse linen, that reached from the neck to the heels. Blincoe was no less terrified at the sight of the pale, lean, sallow-looking multitude, than his nostrils were offended by a dense and heavy smell of rank oil or grease, that arose at their appearance! By comparison, the new comers appeared like so many ladies and gentlemen. On their first entrance, some of the old apprentices took a view of the strangers; but the great bulk first looked after their supper, which consisted of new potatoes, distributed at a hatch door, that opened into the common room from the kitchen. At a signal given, the apprentices rushed to this door, and each, as he made way, received his portion, and withdrew to his place at the table. Blincoe was startled, seeing the boys pull out the fore-part of their shirts, and holding it up with both hands, received the hot boiled potatoes allotted for their supper. The girls, less indecently, if not less filthily, held up their dirty greasy bishops or aprons, that were saturated with grease and dirt, and having received their allowance, scampered off as hard as they could, to their respective places, where, with a keen appetite, each apprentice devoured her allowance, and seemed anxiously to look about for more. Next, the hungry crew ran to the tables of the new comers, and voraciously devoured every crust of bread and every drop of porridge they had left, and put or answered interrogatories as occasion required.

Thus unfavourable were the impressions produced by the scene that presented itself on his first entrance into a cotton-factory. Blincoe was forcibly struck by the absence of that personal cleanliness which had been so rigidly enforced at St. Pancras. The apprentices were required to wash night and morning; but no soap was allowed, and without it, no dirt could be removed. Their tangled locks covered with cotton flue, hung about their persons in long wreaths, floating with every movement. There was no cloth laid on the tables, to which the new comers had been accustomed in the workhouse—no plates, nor knives, nor forks—to be sure the latter utensils were not absolutely necessary with a potatoe-supper. Instead of salt-cellars, as had been allowed at Pancras, a very stingy allowance of salt was laid on the table, and Blincoe saw no other beverage drunk, by the old hands, than pump water.

The supper being devoured, in the midst of the gossiping that ensued, the bell rang, that gave the signal to go to bed. The grim governor entered to take the charge of the newly arrived boys, and his wife, acting the same part by the girls, appeared every way suitable to so rough and unpolished a mate. She was a large grown, robust woman, remarkable for a rough hoarse voice and ferocious aspect. In a surly, heart-chilling tone, she bade the girls follow her. Tremblingly and despondingly the little creatures obeyed, scarcely daring to cast a look at their fellow travellers, or bid them good night. As Blincoe marked the tear to start in their eyes and silently trickle down their cheeks, his heart responsive sank within him. They separated in mournful silence, scarcely a sigh being heard, nor a word of complaint being uttered.

The room in which Blincoe and several of the boys were deposited, was up two pair of stairs. The bed places were a sort of cribs, built in a double tier, all round the chamber. The apprentices slept two in a bed. The beds were of flock. From the quantity of oil imbibed in the apprentices' clothes, and the impurities that accumulated from the oiled cotton, a most disagreeable odour saluted his nostrils. The governor called the strangers to him and allotted to each his bed-place and bed-fellow, not allowing any two of the newly arrived inmates to sleep together. The boy, with whom Blincoe was to chum, sprang nimbly into his berth, and without saying a prayer, or any thing else, fell asleep before Blincoe could undress himself. So completely was he cowed, he could not restrain his tears. He could not forbear execrating the vile treachery of which he felt himself the victim; but still he declared, it never struck him, at least, not till long afterwards, that the *superiors* of St. Pancras had deceived him. The fault, he thought, lay with Messrs. Lamberts, their new masters. When he crept into bed, the stench of the oily clothes and greasy hide of his sleeping comrade, almost turned his stomach.—What, between grief and dismay, and this nauseous smell, it was dawn of day before Blincoe dropt asleep. Over and over again, the poor child repeated every prayer he had been taught, and strove, by unfeigned piety, to recommend himself to the friend of the friendless, and the father of the fatherless. At last, sleep sealed his weary eye-lids—but short was the repose he was allowed to enjoy—before five o'clock, he was awakened by his bed-fellow, who springing upright, at the loud tolling of a bell, told Blincoe to dress with all speed, or the governor would flog him and deprive him of his breakfast. Before Blincoe had time to perform this office, the iron door of the chamber, creaking upon its hinges, was opened, and in came the terrific governor, with the horse-whip in his hand, and every boy hastily tumbled out of his crib, and huddled on his clothes with all possible haste! Blincoe and his fellow travellers were the slowest, not being rightly awake. Blincoe said "bless me, have you *church-service* so soon?" "Church-service, you fool, said one of the larger apprentices, it is to the mill *service* you are called, and you had better look sharp, or you'll catch it!" saying this, off he scampered. Blincoe, who was at first amazed at the trepidation, that appeared in the apprentices, soon understood the cause. The grim-looking governor, with the carbuncled nose, bearing the emblem of arbitrary rule, a horse-whip in his hand, made his appearance, and stalking round the chamber, looked in every bed-place; as he passed Blincoe and his young comrades, he bestowed a withering look upon them, which, fully understanding, they hastened below; arrived there, Blincoe saw some of the boys washing themselves at a pump, and was directed to do the same.—The whole mass sat down to breakfast at five o'clock in the morning. The meal consisted of *black bread* and *blue milk-porridge*. Blincoe and his fellow strangers took their places, mingled with the rest of the apprentices, who, marking their dislike of the bread, eagerly seized every opportunity of eating it themselves. Blincoe and his comrades looked wistfully at each other. Consternation sat deeply imprinted on their features; but every tongue was silent; young as they were, they had sense enough to perceive the necessity of submission and the prudence of reserve.

They reached the mill about half past five.—The water was on, from the bottom to the top, in all the floors, in full movement. Blincoe heard the burring sound before he reached the portals and smelt the fumes of the oil with which the axles of twenty thousand wheels and spindles were bathed. The moment he entered the doors, the noise appalled him, and the stench seemed intolerable.

He did not recollect that either of the Messrs. Lamberts' were present at the mill, on his first entrance. The newly arrived were received by Mr. Baker, the head manager, and by the overlookers of the respective rooms. They were mustered in the making-up room; the boys and girls in separate divisions. After being looked at, and laughed at, they were dispersed in the various floors of the mill, and set to various tasks.—Blincoe was assigned to a room, over which a man named *Smith presided*. The task first allotted to him was, to pick up the loose cotton, that fell upon the floor. Apparently, nothing could be easier, and he set to with diligence, although much terrified by the whirling motion and noise of the machinery, and not a little affected by the dust and flue with which he was half suffocated. They span coarse numbers; unused to the stench, he soon felt sick, and by constantly stooping, his back ached. Blincoe, therefore, took the liberty to sit down; but this attitude, he soon found, was strictly forbidden in cotton mills. His task-master (Smith) gave him to understand, he must keep on his legs. Ho did so, till twelve o'clock, being six hours and a half, without the least intermission.—Blincoe suffered at once by thirst and hunger—the moment the bell rang, to announce dinner, all were in motion to get out as expeditiously as possible. Blincoe ran out amongst the crowd, who were allowed to go—never, in his life, before did he know the value of wholesome air so perfectly. He had been sick almost to fainting, and it revived him instantaneously! The cocknies mingled together, as they made progress towards the apprentice-house! Such as were playsome made to each other! and the melancholy seemed to mingle their tears! When they reached the apprentice-room, each of them had a place assigned at the homely board! Blincoe does not remember of what his dinner consisted; but is perfectly sure, that neither roast beef nor plum-pudding made its appearance—and that the provisions, the cookery, and the mode of serving it out, were all very much below the standard of the ordinary fare of the workhouse in which he had been reared.

During the space of a week or ten days, that Blincoe was kept picking up cotton, he felt at night very great weariness, pains in his back and ancles; and he heard similar complaints from his associates. They might have suffered less had they been taken to the mill at five o'clock, been worked till eight, and then allowed time to eat their breakfast; but six hours' confinement, to close work, no matter of what kind, in an atmosphere as foul as that which circulated in a cotton-mill, is certainly injurious to the health and growth of children of tender years. Even in mills worked by water, and where the temperature of the air is nearly the same within the mill as without, this is the case; but incomparably more so in mills, such as are found in Manchester, where, in many, the average heat is from 70 to 90 degrees of Fahrenheit's scale. After Blincoe had been employed in the way described, he was *promoted* to the more important employment of a roving winder. Being too short of stature, to reach his work, standing on the floor, he was placed on a block; but this expedient only remedied a part of the evil; for he was not able by any possible exertion, to keep pace with the machinery. In vain, the poor child declared it was not in his power to move quicker. He was beaten by the overlooker, with great severity, and cursed and reviled from morning till night, till his life become a burthen to him, and his body discoloured by bruises. In common, with his fellow apprentices, Blincoe was wholly dependent upon the mercy of the overlookers, whom he found, generally speaking, a set of brutal, ferocious, illiterate ruffians, alike void of understanding, as of humanity! Blincoe complained to Mr. Baker, the manager, and all he said to him was:—*"do your work well, and you'll not be beaten."*—It was but seldom, either of the masters visited the mill, and when they did,

Blincoe found it was useless to complain. The overlooker, who had charge of him, had a certain quantity of work to perform in a given time. If every child did not perform his allotted task, the fault was imputed to his overlooker, and he was discharged.—On the other hand, a premium was given, if the full quantity of work was done, and not otherwise. If, therefore, Messrs. Lamberts had remonstrated, or had reprimanded the task-masters, by whom the children were thus mercilessly treated, those task-masters could, and most probably would have said, that if the owners insisted upon so much work being extracted from the apprentices, and a greater quantity of yarn produced, than it was possible to effect by fair and moderate labour, *they must allow them* severity of punishment, to keep the children in a state of continual exertion. Blincoe had not, of course, sense to understand this, the principal, if not the sole cause of the ferocity of the overlookers—but such was, and is the inhuman policy prevailing in cotton-mills, and whilst that cause remains unchanged, the effect inevitably must be the same. Each of the task-masters, to acquire favour and emolument, urged the poor children to the very utmost!—Such is the driving system, which still holds its course, and which leads to the exhaustion and destruction of annual myriads, and to the utmost frightful crimes;—and such is the force of avarice, there are plenty of spinners, so depraved, as not only to sacrifice other people's children, but even *their own*. Blincoe, was not treated with that sanguinary and murderous ferocity in this mill which these pages will soon delineate; but from morning till night, he was continually being beaten, pulled by the hair of his head, kicked or cursed.

It was the custom, in Lowdham Mills, as it is in most water-mills, to make the apprentices work up lost time, by working over hours! a custom, that might not be deemed unreasonable, or found oppressive, if the regular hours were of moderate duration. Blincoe did not say, that this custom was abused at Lowdham Mill, in an equal degree, to what it was in others; but when children of seven years of age, or, by probability, younger, and to work fourteen hours every day in the week, Sundays excepted, any addition was severely felt, and they had to stop at the mill during dinner time, to clean the frames every other day. Once in ten days, or a fortnight, the whole of the finer machinery used to be taken to pieces and cleaned, and then they had to remain at the mill from morning till night, and frequently have been unable to find time to get any food from this early breakfast till night, after they had left off, a term frequently extended from fifteen to sixteen hours incessant labour.

As an inducement to the children to volunteer to work, the whole dinner-hour, a premium of a halfpenny was allowed! Small as was the bribe, it induced many, and Blincoe amongst the number! On such occasions, the dinner was brought up in tin cans, and often has Blincoe's allowance stood till night, whilst he was almost famished with hunger, and he has often carried it back, or rather eaten it on the road, cold, nauseous, and covered with flue.

Being half starved, and cruelly treated by his task-masters—being spotted as a leopard with bruises: and still believing his ill-treatment arose from causes beyond the controul of the parish officers, by whom he had been disposed of to Messrs. Lamberts, Blincoe resolved to attempt an escape,—to beg his way to London,—to lay his case before the overseers and churchwardens of Saint Pancras, and not only claim redress of injuries, but the fulfilment of the grand promises that had been made to him. "I cannot deny," said Blincoe, "that I feel a glow of pride, when I reflect that, at the ago of seven years and a half, I had courage to resent and to resist oppression, and generosity to feel for the sufferings of my helpless associates, not one of whom durst venture to share the peril of the enterprise.—On the other hand," said he, "I must give them the credit for sincerity; for, if any one had been unguarded or perfidious, who knew of my *intended* expedition, I should have been put under such restraint, as would have effectually prevented a successful attempt to run away! I considered my situation so deplorable, and my state of thraldom so intolerable, that death appeared as a lesser evil. I was not wholly ignorant of the sufferings I might have had to encounter, nor that I might perish on the way, from want of food or shelter, and yet I persevered in an effort, in which, of forty fellow-sufferers, not one had courage to join, although many had parents or relatives, to whom to flee for succour, and I had none! So far, young as I was, I calculated upon difficulty, danger and sufferings.—In one thing, only, was I deceived; that error consisted in thinking the evils of my situation intolerable! I had no recollection of calamities so severe, and consequently no standard by which to regulate my judgment. I therefore, rashly determined in my own mind, that my condition admitted of no aggravation,—I was indeed, soon undeceived! I lived, within the short space of four years, to look back with regret to the comparative degree of ease, plenty of food, and of all other good things enjoyed at Lowdham Mill! This sort of knowledge, is, I believe, commonly taught" said Blincoe, "to all the children of misery, as they sink deeper and deeper in woe! The first stage appears the most intolerable; but as they descend, like me, they sink so profoundly in the depths of wretchedness, that in their melancholy progress, those stages and degrees, which, at first, appeared as intolerable, lose all their terrors, in accumulated misery, and the desponding heart, when it takes a retrospective glance at past sufferings, often arraigns its want of patience and fortitude, for murmurings measured by present calamities. Their former condition appeared comfortable! Such was my condition, at a later period, when, to be released from the greater and heavier misery, which I endured at Lowdham, with all its evils, and in the very worst shape, I should have esteemed it as a positive state of happiness." Such was the philosophical reasoning of Robert Blincoe, in 1822. But, to proceed,—steady to his purpose, he embraced the first favourable opportunity of making the projected attempt to escape! He considered his great danger to lie in being retaken on the road between Lowdham and Nottingham; but he knew no other way, and was afraid to make inquiry! When the manager and overlooker of the room he worked in were busy, Blincoe set off, dressed in his working clothes. His progress began in a sort of canter, looking behind him every fifty yards for the first half mile, when, finding he had not been seen or pursued, he continued his rapid flight till he reached Burton, and there, as fate decreed, that flight suddenly terminated; for, as he trotted onwards, a long-shanged, slip-shod tailor, who worked for Lowdham Mill, slid nimbly from his shop-board, which, unfortunately for Blincoe, faced the road, and, placing himself full in the way, with a malicious kind of grin upon his long, lank visage, said "O! young Parson, where art thou running so fast this way?" saying this, he seized him by the hand, and led him very loath into his cottage, and, giving him a seat in the back part of the room, placed himself between his captive and the door.

Blincoe saw, at one glance, by these precautions, that he was caught. His indignation was so great at first, he would not give any answer; noticing which, his false and artful host said to his wife, "Give the young Parson something to eat and drink,—he is weary, and will be better able to pursue his journey, after he has rested and refreshed himself! The Lord commands us to give food to the hungry, and I dare say," addressing himself to him, "thou art not so full, but thou canst eat a bowl of bread and milk." "I must own, to my shame," said Blincoe, "the carnal man, the man of flesh was caught by the bait! I hungered and I ate, and he gave me so much, and I drank so heartily, that my teeth disabled my legs! To be sure, my fare was not very costly:—it consisted of some oaten bread and butter-milk!"

When this sly fox of a tailor found he could eat no more, still blockading the door, to question Blincoe as to the object of his journey, which the latter frankly explained,—"Aye, I thought so," said the detestable hypocrite, "young parson, I thought so,—I saw Satan behind thee, jobbing his prong into thy ****!—I saw thee running headlong into h—ll, when I stept forth to save thee!" This avowal aroused all Blincoe's indignation, and he was determined to have a scuffle with his perfidious host; but he had swallowed so large a portion of butter-milk, and eaten so much oaten bread, he felt he had lost half his speed! Disdainful, however, of fraud or denial, he again avowed his intention, and its cause. The tailor then commenced an harangue upon the deadly sin of a breach of covenant,—assured Blincoe he was acting under the influence of Satan! that he was liable to be sent to Bridewell, to be flogged, and, when sent back to his work, to be debarred of all liberty, and led to and from the mill with a halter round his neck! Blincoe was neither convinced by this reasoning, nor intimidated by these denunciations—but, alas! his gluttonous appetite had disabled him for flight, and being thus disabled, and thus doubly a captive, he made a merit of necessity, and agreed to go back, if his host would be his mediator with Mr. Baker, the manager. This was the precise point to which the jesuitical tailor wished to bring him. Without relinquishing his seat, the treacherous knave doffed his paper cap,

and skeins of thread that still hung round his long, shaggy neck,—
he combed his black, greasy locks, that hung straight as candles
round his lanthorn jaws,—tied a yellow cotton handkerchief round
his neck,—put on a pair of shoes,—took a *crab-tree* stick, full of
knots, in his right hand, and grasping Blincoe's very tight in his
left, he sallied forth on a *work of charity* as the loathsome
hypocrite called his having entrapped and betrayed a poor
oppressed orphan child, fleeing from slavery and oppression. "In
my heart," said Blincoe, "I detested the wretch with greater
bitterness than my task-master; but he held me so tight, I could not
escape—and the sight of the bit of crab-tree which he brandished,
as he chaunted hymns of thanks-giving, had also no small share of
influence in overawing me,—in short, into the counting-house this
second Judas led me. After an admonition to beware how again I
made an attempt of the kind, the manager gave me a severe but not
cruel chastisement." As to the *hospitable* tailor, when he had
delivered him up, he slung away, not waiting to receive Blincoe's
thanks. Whether he took the *five shillings*, which Blincoe was
afterwards told was the standing reward of those who brought back
run-away apprentices, or let it stand till he had five pounds to
receive for such services, he cannot ascertain; but he was told, this
peeping Tom of Burton, had rendered many a poor child the same
sort of kindness. "In consequence of this scurvy trick," said
Blincoe, "I have never been able to conquer the aversion it created
against Methodists; although I am bound to believe, the wretch
was one of the myriads of *counterfeits*, who flock to their standard
from venal and corrupt motives."

After Blincoe had received his punishment, every weal and
bruise with which he had started found a fellow. He was handed
back to Smith, his task-master, by whom he was laughed at and
jeered unmercifully, and worked with an increase of severity.
When Blincoe left work, his old associates flocked around him,
condoling his misfortune, and offering him half-pence and bits of
bread that they had saved! When they heard how *godly* had caught
him, their indignation swelled to such a height, they declared they
would drown him in the mill-dam, if ever they had an opportunity.
These condolements were grateful to his wounded pride and
disappointed hopes. As he retired to his miserable bed, the
governor, grinning horribly, made him a low bow in the military

style, and gave him a hearty kick on his *seat of honour* at the same instant. In this manner, was he ushered to his bed, laughed at by that portion of the elder apprentices, who had made similar attempts, and had undergone a similar or more vindictive punishment. Having abandoned all thoughts of escape, Blincoe submitted sullenly and patiently to his fate;—he worked according to his age and stature, as hard as any one in the mill. When his strength failed, and his limbs refused their office, he endured the strap or the stick, the cuff or the kick, with as much resignation as any of his fellow-sufferers. In the faded complexions, and sallow looks of his associates, he could see, as, in a mirror, his own altered condition! Many of his comrades had, by this time, been more or less injured by the machinery. Some had the skin scraped off the knuckles, clean to the bone, by the fliers; others a finger crushed, a joint or two nipped off in the cogs of the spinning-frame wheels! When his turn to suffer came, the fore-finger of his left hand was caught, and almost before he could cry out, off was the first joint—his lamentations excited no manner of emotion in the spectators, except a coarse joke—he clapped the mangled joint, streaming with blood, to the finger, and ran off to Burton, to the surgeon, who, very composedly put the parts together again, and sent him back to the mill. Though the pain was so intense, he could scarcely help crying out every minute, he was not allowed to leave the frame. He said but little to any one; but was almost continually bemoaning in secret the cruelty of his fate. Before he was eight years old, Blincoe declared, that many a time he had been tempted to throw himself out of one of the upper windows of the factory— but when he came to look at the leap he purposed taking, his courage failed him—a propensity, he mentioned not as thinking it evinced any commendable feeling, but as an illustration of the natural and unavoidable consequences of working children too hard, and subjecting them to so many severe privations.

About the second year of his servitude, when the whole of the eighty children sent from Pancras Workhouse, had lost their plump and fresh appearance, and acquired the pale and sickly hue which distinguished factory children from all others, a most deplorable accident happened in Lowdham Mill, and in Blincoe's presence. A girl, named Mary Richards, who was thought remarkably handsome when she left the workhouse, and, who might be nearly or quite ten years of age, attended a drawing frame, below which, and about a foot from the floor, was a horizontal shaft, by which the frames above were turned. It happened, one evening, when most of her comrades had left the mill, and just as she was taking off the weights, her apron was caught by the shaft. In an instant the poor girl was drawn by an irresistible force and dashed on the floor. She uttered the most heart rending shrieks! Blincoe ran towards her, an agonized and helpless beholder of a scene of horror that exceeds the power of my pen to delineate! He saw her whirled round and round with the shaft—he heard the bones of her arms, legs, thighs, &c. successively snap asunder, crushed, seemingly, to atoms, as the machinery whirled her round, and drew tighter and tighter her body within the works, her blood was scattered over the frame and streamed upon the floor, her head appeared dashed to pieces—at last, her mangled body was jammed in so fast, between the shafts and the floor, that the water being low and the wheels off the gear, it stopped the main shaft! When she was extricated, every bone was found broken!—her head dreadfully crushed!—her clothes and mangled flesh were, apparently incxtricably mixed together, and she was carried off, as supposed, quite lifeless. "I cannot describe," said Blincoe, "my sensations at this appalling scene. I shouted out aloud for them to stop the wheels! When I saw her blood thrown about like water from a twirled mop, I fainted." But neither the spine of her back was broken, nor were her brains injured, and to the amazement of every one, who beheld her mangled and horrible state, by the skill of the surgeon, and the excellence of her constitution, she was saved!—Saved to what end? the philosopher might ask—to be sent back to the same mill, to pursue her labours upon crutches, made a cripple for life, without a shilling indemnity from the parish, or the owners of the mill! Such was the fate of this poor girl, but, dismal as it was, it will be seen by the succeeding parts of this narrative, that a lot still more horrible awaited many of her fellow-sufferers, whom the parish officers of St. Pancras, pursuant to Acts of Parliament authority, had apprenticed for fourteen years to the masters of Lowdham Cotton Mill. The dreadful spectacle Blincoe had witnessed in the racking of Mary Richards, rendered his employment more odious than ever.

It is already stated, that the food was very ordinary and not very plentiful; the apprentices were so oppressed by hunger, that the oldest and most daring sallied out at night and plundered the fields, and frequent complaints were made, and the apprentices got a very bad name, which belonged rather to the masters, in whose parsimony it originated!

When Blincoe had served about three years of his time, an event happened at Lowdham Mill, arising out of the manner in which apprentices were treated, that wrought a complete revolution there, and led to a new era in Blincoe's biography! Among the girls, who were bound apprentices to Messrs. Lamberts of Nottingham and Lowdham, were two sisters, named Fanny and Mary Collier, who had a mother residing in London. These young girls finding their health declining from excess of labour, bad provisions, and want of wholesome air and exercise, found means to write a letter to their mother, full of complaints, upon which, the widow undertook a journey to Lowdham, where she resided a fortnight, during which time, she was a reserved and shrewd observer of the condition of her own and of other children, and then returned to the metropolis. As far as Blincoe remembers these circumstances, Mrs. Collier did not make any complaints to Messrs. Lamberts, or to the manager! She reserved such representation for the parish officers of Saint Pancras, which induced them to send down a parochial committee, to inquire into the state and condition of the apprentices. One day, just as the dinner was being served out in the *usual* slovenly manner, without the least notice of the intended visit having been previously given, the Committee arrived, without asking or waiting for permission, they walked into the common room, and tasting the viands upon the table, they found them such as had been described. Whether *conscience* had any concern in the effort to discover and reform abuses in the mill, said Blincoe, I know not; but this I do know, that, if they had had a spark of shame, pity or remorse, the sallow, and sickly appearance of the eighty victims, saying nothing of Mary Richards, who was for ever rendered a cripple, ought to have filled them with sorrow and shame, on account of the base and cruel imposition, that had been practised in 1799. It is more probable, however, that the atrocious treatment experienced by the thousands and tens of thousands of orphan children, poured forth from our charitable institutions, and from parish workhouses, and the dreadful rapidity with which they were consumed in the various cotton-mills, to which they were transported, and the sad spectacle exhibited by most of the survivors, were the real causes, which, in 1802, produced Sir Robert Peel's Bill, for the relief and protection of infant paupers employed in cotton-mills. Hence, the extraordinary liveliness evinced by the overseers and churchwardens of Saint Pancras might have been occasioned by the dreadful scenes of cruelty and oppression developed during the progress of that Bill, which Blincoe never heard of, nor ever saw, till eleven or twelve years after it had passed into a law. It would be difficult to produce a more striking instance of the utter contempt, in which the upstart owners of great establishments treated an act, purposely enacted to restrain their unparalled cruelty and waste of human life. The act itself declared the masters, owners, or occupiers of every cotton-mill in Great Britain and Wales should have a legible copy of the act, placed in some conspicuous and public part of each mill, and accessible to every one; yet, Blincoe, who was reared in the cotton-mill, never saw or heard of any such law, till eleven or twelve years after it had been enacted! When the committee began their investigation, as to the treatment and condition of the children sent from St. Pancras Workhouse, Blincoe was called up among others and admonished to speak the truth and nothing but the truth! So great however was the terror of the stick and strap, being applied to their persons, after these great dons should be at a great distance, it rendered him, and no doubt the great majority of his fellow sufferers extremely cautious and timid. It is however, likely, that their looks bespoke their sufferings, and told a tale not to be misunderstood. The visitors saw their food, dress, bedding, and they caused, in conjunction with the local magistrate, very great alterations to be made. A new house was ordered to be erected near the mill, for the use of the apprentices, in which there were fewer beds to a given space. The quantity of good and wholesome animal food to be dressed and distributed in a more decent way, was specified. A much more cleanly and decorous mode of cookery and serving up the dinner and other meals was ordered. The apprentices were divided into six classes, and a new set of tin cans, numbered 1, 2, 3, 4, 5, and 6, were made, to be served up to each individual, according to the class to which he or she may belong, to hold the soup or porridge! The old governor was discharged, who had given them all such a fright on their first arrival, and several of the overlookers were dismissed and new ones introduced;—among the latter description of persons was a man, who seemed wholly destitute of humanity—his name was William Woodward—born, I believe, at Cromford, in Derbyshire. The appearance of this ferocious tyrant at Lowdham Mill proved a much heavier curse, scourge and affliction to Blincoe, than all the grievances which had existed, or were removed! As Woodward's amusement, in tormenting these poor apprentices, will occupy a large space in the next chapter, I shall say little of him in this.

It was the ill fortune of Blincoe and his associates, that, shortly after the reforms specified were introduced, and the hours of labour reduced, so that their situation became every way incomparably more eligible, Lowdam Mill stopped working.

At this period, Blincoe had served about four years of his time, and had learnt to wind rovings, and spin at the throstle, and certainly earned as much money for his master in the week as would suffice to keep him a month or longer, in meat, drink and clothes; but he had not been instructed in any part of the stocking-trade, nor had he acquired such a degree of knowledge of the cotton-spinning, as might enable him to gain his bread elsewhere.

At this juncture, if justice had been done, the apprentices would have reverted to Saint Pancras parish, and not been abandoned as they were, and turned over to a new master, without any care being taken, that he should, if he took them, abide by the condition specified in their first indentures, and act up to the regulations introduced at Lowdham Mill.

Blincoe said, he believed the Messrs. Lamberts wrote to the parish officers of Saint Pancras, informing them of the situation of the children, in order that their friends might take back whom they pleased to claim, and if, in this conclusion, Blincoe is right, and these officers neglected to take proper measures for the safety and protection of so large a body of children, as they had sent to Lowdham Mill, all healthy and straight limbed, they are morally responsible for the unparalled sufferings to which they were afterwards exposed. When the subject shall again come before parliament, it will be requisite to have the conduct of the parish officers on this occasion thoroughly investigated, not so much from a wish to have their offences visited with any legal penalty, if such were practicable, as to shew the necessity of abrogating the power invested in them by act of parliament, to place children beyond a given distance from the place of their birth or settlement:—and secondly, to deprive them altogether of the power of tearing away children from their parents, and sending them into any manufactories whatever, without the knowledge and consent of their parents, or next of kin. If the parish officers think proper to apprentice them to any of the ordinary and established trades, they ought to have that power independently of their parents. In the mill, where Blincoe was next consigned, the *parish children* were considered, treated, and *consumed as a part of the raw materials*; their strength, their marrow, their lives, were consumed and converted into money! and as their livestock consisting of parish apprentices, diminished, new flocks of victims arrived from various quarters, without the cost of purchase to supply their place!

It is within the compass of probability, that there have been, and are yet, instances, wherein the overseers of the poor, and more especially the *assistant* overseers, who are mere mercenaries, and serve for pay, have been, and are, some of them at least, *bribed* by the owners of mills for spinning silk, cotton or woollen yarn, to visit the habitation of the persons receiving parochial aid, and to compel them, when children are wanting, utterly regardless of education, health, or inclination, to deliver up their offspring, or by cutting off the parish allowance leave them to perish for want!

When Messrs. Lamberts gave up the cotton-yarn establishment, carried on at Lowdham Mill, they permitted all their apprentices who wished to leave their employment in a cotton-mill, to write to their parents and friends, and some few found redeemers; the great bulk were, unhappily left to their fate! Being a foundling, and knowing no soul on earth to whom he could look up for succour, Robert Blincoe was one of the unhappy wretches, abandoned to as dismal a destiny as ever befel *a parish apprentice*. It was his evil fortune, with a multitude of fellow sufferers, to be turned over *en masse* to Mr. ELLICE NEEDHAM, of Highgate Wall, Derbyshire, the master and owner of Litton Mill, near Tideswell.

35

Before, however, I close this delineation of the character and conduct of the owners of Lowdham Cotton-Mill—Messrs. William, Charles, and Thomas Lambert—it is due to them, if living, whatever may be their fortune, and to their memory, if deceased, to state, that, with the exception of Mary Richards, who was so dreadfully racked upon a shaft, and her bones mostly broken, not one of the children sent to their mill by St. Pancras parish, were injured as to be made a cripple, nor were they deformed in their knees and ancles. That there were deficiencies as to food and an excess of labour exacted, is clear, by the alterations which were introduced; but still, compared with what they soon afterwards suffered, they were humanely treated.

They were kept decently clad, had a bettermost suit reserved for Sundays and holidays—were occasionally allowed a little time for play, in the open air, and upon *Goose fair-day*, which is, or then was, a great festival at Nottingham—the whole of them were conveyed in carts to that celebrated place, and regaled with furmety, and sixpence in money was allowed to the very youngest! They went pretty regularly to Lowdham Church on Sundays; were not confined within gates and walls, as was the case at most other mills, where parish apprentices were immured! nor were there any iron-bars before the windows! They were *worked hard*; but not so hard as to distort their limbs, nor occasion declines or deaths! Their food latterly was good, and cleanly cooked. Their bedding, though coarse, was clean! When they had meat, they were allowed trenchers, knives, forks and spoons. It will presently be seen, when carried away from Lowdham Mill, into what a den of vice, disease and famine, filth and slavery, they were plunged; by what hellions they were worried, and all in defiance of a positive, and recently made law, on purpose for their protection, and in the face of the VISITING MAGISTRATE whose visits were, according to Blincoe's assertion, too frequently directed to the luxurious table of the master, to admit even a chance of justice to the apprentices. May this exposition of crimes and suffering inflicted upon the friendless, the orphan, the widow's son, induce honest and upright men, senators and legislators, effectually to curb the barbarous propensities of hard-hearted masters, and rescue their nation from a worse stain, than even the African Slave Trade, horrible as was that odious traffic, ever inflicted.

CHAPTER IV.

The next cotton mill to which poor Blincoe was consigned, together, with those of his companions in tribulation, who had no friend to redeem them, from impending misery, belonged to a Mr. Ellice Needham. Like most of his fraternity, his origin was obscure. He is said to have arisen from an abject state of poverty, and had it been by honourable industry, his prosperous fortune had redounded to his credit. Of his primeval state of poverty, it was his weakness to be ashamed. By the profusion of his table, and the splendour and frequency of his entertainments, he seemed to wish to cover and conceal his mean descent. His house, lawns, equipage, and style of living, completely eclipsed the neighbouring gentry; yet, boundless was his ostentation, he was in his heart sordidly mean and parsimonious. His cruelty, in wringing from poor friendless orphans, the means of supporting his guilty and unbecoming pomp, sufficiently evinces the baseness of his heart! His mansion, in 1803, and years later, was at Highgate Wall, near Buxton in Derbyshire.

To this arrogant and unfeeling master, Messrs. Lambert made over the unexpired term of years for which the greater part of the parish apprentices had been bound by their respective indentures. What premium was paid, or, if any, I know not. As this master was neither a hosier, nor a lace manufacturer, he had not the power to fulfil the conditions imposed on Messrs. Lamberts, viz. to instruct the girls, during the last three years of their time, in lace-knitting, and the boys in stocking-weaving. The consequence was, the poor children lost those important advantages, and those who survived the term of their apprenticeship to Ellice Needham, found themselves without that degree of skill which was requisite to enable them to gain their bread, in almost any other cotton-mill, and could touch none but the very coarsest work.

As Messrs. Lamberts were constrained, by circumstances, to stop their works, it might be, that they had not means to support the apprentices; but were forced to get rid of them with the utmost expedition. There have been instances, where, in case of Bankruptcy, parish apprentices bound to cotton-masters, have been put into carts, driven to the verge of the parish, and there turned adrift without money—without a friend or a place to shelter them. According to Blincoe's account, although Messrs. Lamberts' informed the guardians of the poor of St. Pancras parish of the necessity they were under of giving up their apprentices, or turning them over to their masters, no steps were taken for the protection of the friendless children, an imputation, the more extraordinary, when the promptitude and decision with which they had acted in the case recited, is considered. It is, therefore, probable, that their activity might be owing to the horrid tales, that had then burst upon the public, descriptive of the cruelty and misery, of which parish children placed out in cotton-mills were the victims. It was in 1802, that Sir Robert Peel, of Bury, who had the largest number of parish and foundling children, employed in his cotton-mills, of any cotton-master in Great Britain, brought forward his bill for their protection. According to Blincoe's narrative, the committee from St. Pancras arrived at Lowdham Mill, at this juncture, and the reforms introduced at Lowdham Mill, were, therefore, likely to have been owing to the parliamentary agitation of that question; and nothing can be more highly illustrative of the force of public opinion, than this proof of its potent effect on the officers of St. Pancras parish!—Supposing the conjecture to be well founded, at the time the apprentices were removed from Lowdham Mill, this humane act had passed into a law, and had become all but a dead-letter!—It may also have been a reliance upon the effect of that law which induced the parish officers to leave the children to their fate—what THAT fate was will presently appear!

It seems, that Mr. Ellice Needham, the master of Litton Mill, went to Lowdham, to inspect the condition of the apprentices, who had improved very materially after the introduction of the new regulations. Nothing could be more kind or condescending than Ellice Needham's deportment at Lowdham. To some, he gave money—to all, he promised most liberal and kind usage—he promised like a Titus—but he performed like a Caligula.

Blincoe could not recollect, with precision, the number of apprentices, male and female, who were removed in carts from Lowdham to Litton Mill. The first day's progress brought them to Cromford, where they halted for the night. The girls were lodged in dwelling-houses; the boys, on straw, in a barn or stable! The next morning, the whole party were marched on foot through the village, as far as Matlock toll-bar, so proud was Woodward (their conductor) of their healthy appearance! Here they again mounted their carts! But this improvement is not imputable to the wholesomeness of cotton-factory employment; but to the effect of the recent modifications introduced at Lowdham Mill, and to their diminished hours of toil.

It was in the gloomy month of November, when this removal took place! On the evening of the second day's journey, the devoted children reached Litton Mill. Its situation, at the bottom of a sequestered glen, and surrounded by rugged rocks, remote from any human habitation, marked a place fitted for the foul crimes of frequent occurrence which hurried so many of the friendless victims of insatiate avarice, to an untimely grave.

The savage features of the adjacent scenery impressed a general gloom upon the convoy, when Woodward pointed out to them the lonely mill to which they were travelling. As the hands were then at work, all of whom, except the overlookers, were parish children, the conductor of the new comers led them through the mill. The effect of the review filled the mind of Blincoe, and perhaps his unhappy associates, with deep dismay. The pallid, sickly complexions—the meagre, haggard appearance of the Litton Mill apprentices, with their filthy and ragged condition, gave him a sorrowful foretaste of the dismal fate that apparently awaited him. From the mill, they were escorted to the 'prentice-house, where every thing wore a discouraging aspect. Their first meal was water-porridge and oaten cakes—the former thin and ill-made—the latter, baked in flat cakes, on iron griddles, about an inch thick—and being piled up in heaps, was liable to heat, ferment and grow mouldy. This was a new and not a very palatable diet. Whilst Blincoe and many of his comrades went supperless to bed, their half-starved comrades, the Litton Mill apprentices, ravenously devoured what the more dainty Lowdham children turned from with loathing, and told them *their stomachs* would come to in a few days, and that they would be glad to pick from a dunghill, the mouldiest pieces, then so disdainfully flung away.

The lodging-room, the bedding, every thing was inferior to what it was at Lowdham; and the smell, from oil and filth, incomparably more offensive. Blincoe passed a restless night, bitterly deploring his hard destiny, and trembling at the thought of greater sufferings! Soon after four in the morning, they were summoned to the work, by the ringing of a bell. Blincoe was put to wind rovings. He soon found an immense difference, in his situation, having much more work to perform, and being treated with a brutal severity, hitherto unknown to him.

Blincoe remarked, that few of the apprentices had either knife, fork, or spoon, to use at table, or hats, shoes, or stockings. At Lowdham, particularly during the latter part of their stay there, the children used to wash at the pump, night and day, and were allowed soap! At Litton mill, they were called out so early, and worked so late, that little or no attention was given to personal cleanliness! On Friday night, the apprentices were washed, combed, and shirted! Blincoe found his companions in a woeful condition—their bodies were literally covered with weals and contusions—their heads full of wounds, and, in many cases, lamentably, infested with vermin! The eldest girls had to comb and wash the younger apprentices—an irksome task, which was carelessly and partially performed. No soap was allowed—a small quantity of meal was given as a substitute; and this from the effects of keen hunger, was generally eaten. The first day's labour at Litton Mill, convinced Blincoe, into what a den of vice and misery he was cast. The overlookers were fierce and brutal, beyond any thing he had ever witnessed at Lowdham Mill; to which servitude, terrible as it once appeared, he looked back with regret. In the retrospect of his own conduct, he felt shame and sorrow—for, compared with what he had to perform and to endure, he now considered that he had lived in idleness and luxury at Lowdham. The custom of washing and shifting on Friday night, arose, he said from a notion, that it was more *profitable* to allow those ablutions to be then performed, that the apprentices might be kept to work till *midnight* on Saturday, or even beyond that hour. The apprentices slept about fifty in a room. The governor used to unlock the door of each room when the first bell rang: having unlocked the last room door, he went back to the first, with a switch stick in his hand, and if he found any one in bed, or slowly dressing, he used to lay on without mercy; by which severity, the rooms were soon empty. The apprentices had their breakfast generally of water-porridge, called in this part of Derbyshire "stir-pudding," and oaten cake, which they took in the mill. The breakfast hour was eight o'clock; but the machinery did not stop, and so irregular were their meals, it sometimes did not arrive till ten or eleven o'clock. At other times, the overlookers would not allow the apprentices to eat it, and it stood till it grew cold and covered with flue! Skim-milk, or butter-milk was allowed; but very sparingly, and often in a stinking state, when it was served out. Forty minutes were allowed for dinner; of which time, full one half was absorbed in cleaning the frames. Sometimes the overlookers detained them in the mill the whole dinner-time, on which occasion, a halfpenny was given, or rather promised. On those occasions, they had to work the whole day through, generally *sixteen hours, without rest or food*! These excessive labours, accompanied by comparative starvation, may appear to my reader, as, at first, it did to me, *incredible*; but Blincoe's relations, marvellous as it may appear, was afterwards confirmed by individuals, whose narratives *will be given*, and with whom no sort of acquaintance or intercourse had latterly subsisted. Owing to this shamefully protracted time of labour, to the ferocity with which the children were driven by stripes, cuffs, and kicks, and to the insufficiency of food, no less than its bad and unwholesome quality. Blincoe, in common with his fellow-sufferers has often dropped down at the frames, and been so weary, when, at last, he left work, he has given a stronger boy a halfpenny, or a part of his supper, to allow him to lean upon him on his way back to the 'prentice-house.

Bad as was the food, the cookery was still worse.—The most inferior sort of Irish-fed bacon was purchased for the consumption of these children, and this boiled with turnips, put into the water, I cannot say without washing; but certainly without paring!—Such was the *Sunday* fare of the parish children at Litton Mill. When first Blincoe, and the rest of the children arrived from Lowdham, they noticed many of the other apprentices had neither spoon nor knife; but had to eat as they could, meat, thick-porridge, or broth, nor were the new comers long allowed any such implements. On Sunday, bacon-broth and turnips were served out, which they eat with oaten-cake, in dirty wooden bowls. It could not be otherwise, than unpalatable; for the portion of water to be converted into *broth*, was very ample. In this, rusty, half putrid, fish-fed bacon, and unpaired turnips were boiled!—A portion of this broth, with coarse oaten-cake was served out, as the first course of a frequent Sunday's dinner. Next, the rusty bacon was portioned out with the boiled unpared turnips!—There was generally, a large quantity of broth to spare, which often became very fetid before it was cold. Into this stuff, no better than hog-wash, a few pails more of water were poured and some meal stirred in, and the disgusting mess was served out for supper or the next day's breakfast, as circumstances required. Blincoe declared, that the stench of this broth was often so powerful as to turn his stomach, and yet, bad as it was, keen hunger forced him to eat it. From all those and other sources of sickness and disease, no one will be surprised that contagious fevers arose in the mill; nor that the number of deaths should be such as to require frequent supplies of parish children, to fill up the vacancies. That such numerous draughts made from mills, where there was no increase of building or of machinery, or apparent call for more infant labourers should not have caused parish officers to institute inquiry, as to the fate of their predecessors, goes far toward confirming the worst imputations cast by the surviving sufferers, upon their parochial guardians. The evidence given by Sir Robert Peel and others, before parliamentary committees, will throw still further light on this important subject, and prove how generally the offspring of the poor have been abandoned by their legal guardians, and left at the disposal of greedy and unfeeling sons of traffic. This neglect on the part of parish officers, was the producing cause of many of the avaricious cotton-masters escaping punishment, for offences which richly merited the gallows. Contagious disease, fatal to the apprentices, and dangerous to society, was the degree of magnitude, at which, the independent rich, more, perhaps, from selfish than social feelings, took alarm, and the public prints exposed a part of the existing abuses in cotton-mills, of which parish children were the victims. So horrid were these recitals, and so general and loud the indignation which they excited, that it reached the inmost recesses of the flinty hearts of the great cotton-masters. Their fears taught them mercy, when no longer able to withstand, nor to silence the accusations brought against them by public-spirited and disinterested opponents. Some of the greatest delinquents yielded, and even became advocates for the interference of the legislative power, between themselves and their servants. A reference to the Appendix will shew that they were accused by the genuine friends of humanity of aiming, by this concession, to insinuate themselves into the confidence of their opponents, and thereby neutralize and subdue the fine spirit by which they found their grasping, vile, insatiate avarice controlled. Be this as it may, those individuals who took so much pains to obtain the act of 1802, seem to have given themselves no manner of trouble, to see it enforced. Almost before the first year expired, it was considered a dead-letter. Just at this crisis, the cruelties, exercised on apprentices at Litton Mill, were at their height. Excess of toil, of filth, and of hunger, led to the poor children being visited by contagious fevers. This calamity, which often broke, by premature death, the bands of this vile thraldom, prevailed to such an extent, as to stop the works. At last, such was Blincoe's declaration, he had known forty boys sick at once, being a fourth of the whole number employed in the mill. From the combined testimony of many apprentices, none were considered sick, till it was found impossible, by menaces or by corporeal punishment, to keep them to their work. The medical gentlemen, who sometimes attended the sick, aware of the cause of the deaths, used to say, and like a sensible man he spoke:—"It is not drugs, but kitchen physic they want:" and his general prescription was plenty of good bread, beef, soup and mutton broth. When I questioned Blincoe and others, why this medical man did not represent the horrid plight they were in to the magistrates, he said, the surgeon and magistrates were friends and guests of the master, and in the frequent habit of feasting with him! Blincoe was among the number of the sick, and remembers pitch, tobacco, &c. being burnt in the chamber, and vinegar sprinkled on their beds and on the floor. Circumstances which sufficiently denote the malignity of the disease, and the serious apprehensions that were entertained. So great has the mortality been, that Mr. Needham felt it adviseable to divide the burials, and a part of the dead were buried in Tadington Church-yard, although the burial fees were double the charge of those at Tideswell. Notwithstanding this extraordinary degree of sickness and mortality, Blincoe declares that the local magistracy took no manner of notice of these occurrences!!!

It might be hazardous to trust so far to the memory, the integrity, or the judgment of Blincoe, or to affirm that the conduct of the local magistrates really was thus culpable—but the imputation is corroborated by the total silence of the magistrates of this part of Derbyshire, as to the character and conduct of the owners of Litton Mill, during the parliamentary investigation of 1816, 17, 18, 19. The concurrent testimony of Blincoe and several of his fellow-sufferers confirm the fact of contagious fevers having occurred in this mill; of the numerous deaths it occasioned; of the consequent division of the funerals; and of the remarks of the clergyman, by whom the last sad rites were performed; and also, that, *once*, there was a Coroner's inquest held! there exists some difference of opinion, as to the material fact, whether the body had not been first deposited in the earth, and afterwards taken up. Not a spark of pity was shewn to the sick of either sex: they were worked to the very last moment it was possible for them to work: and when it was no longer possible, if they dropped down, they were put into a wheel-barrow, and wheeled to the 'prentice-house. According to Blincoe's statement, they were left in the common room below, or carried to their berth in the bed-room, and there left to live or die! In this melancholy state, all the change that took place in the diet, was an allowance of some *treacle-tea*, that is, hot water sweetened with treacle. The doctor was seldom called, till the patient was in the agonies of death. Generally speaking, the dying experienced less attention than a sheep or a hog! The owner of Litton Mill was more tender to those animals; because they cost money, and the anxiety of a character like Mr. Needham's could only be excited by the prospect of a loss of capital! This solicitude was proportioned to the extent of that risk; and as parish children and destitute orphans could be had at a less price than sheep or pigs, to supply the place of those that died, it followed, that they were less thought of. I would not willingly exaggerate the atrocities I am depicting. I would not act so unwisely as to overcharge the picture I am drawing; and it is with some degree of diffidence, I state, in consequence of combined and positive testimony, that no nurses or *nursing* was allowed to the sick, further than what one invalid could do for another! That neither candle nor lamp-light was allowed, nor the least sign of sympathy or regret manifested! These facts I admit, are so repugnant to every feeling of Christian charity, that they wear the aspect of greatly embellished truths, or what is but little worse, of malignant fabrications. If they are such, the fault is not mine; for repeatedly, and in the most impressive manner in my power, I admonished Blincoe and his fellow-sufferers, to abstain from falsehood, telling him and them, it would be sure to be detected and lead to their disgrace. What I thought might have more influence with such persons, I also urged the triumph, such baseness on their part, could confer on the master cotton spinners, most distinguished by cruelty and tyranny; yet, still Blincoe and the whole of his former comrades perseveringly and consistently adhered to the truth of the horrid imputations, and declared, if they were called upon, they would at any time confirm their statement. I was bound to give them publicity—if they are founded in truth. If their great features are correctly delineated, no lapse of time ought to be allowed to shelter the delinquents. They should be brought to a public trial; for the imputations extend to too many acts of torture and of wilful deliberate murder; and to the indulgence of propensities, as to overpower scepticism. They embrace atrocities exercised upon poor and friendless boys and girls, of a nature no less abominable than the worst of those which apply to that disgrace to womanhood, Elizabeth Brownrig, or more recently, to the unhappy culprit, Governor Wall. There are yet living, perhaps a hundred witnesses who have been partakers of these ferocious inflictions. Many of them, though in the prime of life, are reduced to such a state of decrepitude, as to flash conviction upon the most incredulous, that it could have resulted from nothing but the most unexampled and long continued cruelty. From the continued and relentless exercise of unlimited despotism upon the truly insulted and most friendless of human beings, upon those, for whose especial protection, a law had been then recently enacted, which, had it been enforced, would have efficiently prevented the occurrence of these crimes, and if I were to assert, that it would be difficult, if not impossible, from the record of sufferings inflicted upon Negro slaves, to quote instances of greater atrocity, than what I have, or am about to develope, I should not exaggerate, nor should I be guilty of bombast, were I to affirm, that the national character has been, and is seriously dishonoured by that system of boundless commercial avarice, in which these detestable crimes originated. It will continue thus shaded, till a full and fair investigation takes place. There never yet was a crisis, when, in the commercial world, the march of avarice was so rapid, or its devastations so extensive upon the morals and well being of society, as within the period embraced by this narrative; a march that seems to acquire celerity in proportion to the increasing spread of its malific *influence*, and to derive *impunity* from the prodigious wealth it accumulates in the hands of a few great and unfeeling capitalists, at the expence of the individual happiness, health, and morals of the million. This iniquitous system is the prolific parent of that tremendous flood of vice, which has saturated the manufacturing populace, with the most appalling depravity. This has reduced those many hundred thousand weavers, to a state of destitution so extreme, as to render the condition of the most destitute portion, incomparably worse than that of the field-slave in the West India plantations, who has the good fortune to belong to a humane proprietor. This baleful and wide wasting system throws upon the crown the undeserved odium of being the cause or the abettor of these dreadful evils, by which the poor weaver is oppressed—an impression that has neutralized the loyalty of myriads, and fitted them to become, in the hands of unprincipled demagogues, the source of popular commotions, of foul and iniquitous conspiracies, of deep and radical disloyalty. So indurated, so inveterate, is the loathing and aversion cherished towards the executive government, in all its ramifications, by a large portion of weavers, that it has induced multitudes wholly to renounce, to vilify in every practicable manner, to degrade christianity! I do not, in this declamation, indulge in light, personal, or selfish motives; for whatever I assert, as positive matter of fact, I hold myself morally responsible, and stand publicly pledged to substantiate my assertion, by adducing, if requisite, not alone the authorities on which I make them, but also to *prove* the validity of those authorities.

With this digression, I close the present chapter.—In those that follow there will be found a narrative of crimes which cannot fail to excite, in an equal degree, horror and incredulity:—at the recital of acts of wanton, premeditated, gross, and brutal cruelty, scarcely to be equalled in the annals of the Inquisitorial tribunals of Portugal or Spain; yet all those acts of murder and wanton cruelties, have been perpetrated by a solitary master cotton-spinner, who, though perhaps one of the worst of his tribe, did not stand alone; as will be shewn by evidence that it cannot be successfully rebutted. Nor was it to be expected that the criminality of that master spinner could fail to produce corresponding depravity amongst the wretched apprentices subjected to his rude and savage dominion. In the eventful life of W—— Pitt, the depth and extent of that depravity will be strikingly illustrated!—It will be seen that acts of felony were committed in the vicinity of Litton Mill, by the parish apprentices, not, if I am rightly informed, from *dishonest intention*; but from a desire to be transported to Botany Bay; deeming even that alternative preferable to the endurance of the horrors of the servitude, to which, as parish apprentices, they had been consigned.

CHAPTER V.

Recurring to the description, given to me by Robert Blincoe, of the dreadful state of thraldom, in which, with a multitude of juvenile companions, he was involved at Litton Mill, I am instructed to say, that as excessive toil, the want of proper time for rest, and of nourishing wholesome food, gave rise to contagious disease, so a liberal supply of good provisions and a cessation from toil, quickly restored many to health; instead of taking warning by the results of these terrible examples, no sooner were the invalids sent back to the mill, than the system of over-toil, of boundless cruelty, starvation and torture, was at once resumed. Let it not however be supposed, that any thing in the shape of dainties had been dispensed to the sick. Wheaten bread, coarse pieces of beef boiled down in soup, or mutton for broth, with good milk or butter-milk, sparingly distributed, formed the extent of those indulgences. This diet, luxurious as it was considered in Litton Mill, did not surpass the ordinary standard of the daily fare, that Blincoe had enjoyed at St. Pancras workhouse, and also, during the latter period of his stay at Lowdham Mill.

I have not yet done more than to mention the cuffs, kicks, or scourging, to which, in common with many other of his unhappy comrades, Blincoe stood exposed, since, by his account, almost from the first hour in which he entered the Mill, till he arrived at a state of manhood, it was one continued round of cruel and arbitrary punishment. Blincoe declared, he was so frequently and immoderately beaten, it became quite familiar; and if its frequency did not extinguish the sense of feeling, it took away the terror it excited on his first entrance into this den of ignorance and crime. I asked him if he could state an average number of times in which he thought he might in safety say, he had suffered corporeal punishment in a week. His answer invariably was, that his punishments were so various and so frequent, it was impossible to state with any thing approaching to accuracy. If he is to be credited, during his ten years of hard servitude, his body was never free from contusions, and from wounds inflicted by the cruel master whom he served, by his sons, or his brutal and ferocious and merciless overlookers.

It is already stated, that he was put to the back of a stretching-frame, when he was about eleven years of age, and that often, owing to the idleness, or the absence of the stretcher, he had his master's work, as well as his own to perform. The work being very coarse, the motion was rapid, and he could not keep up to the ends. For this he was sure to be unmercifully punished, although, they who punished him knew the task assigned was beyond what he could perform. There were different stretchers in the mill; but, according to Blincoe's account, they were all of them base and ferocious ruffians. Robert Woodward, who had escorted the apprentices from Lowdham Mill, was considered the worst of those illiterate vulgar tyrants. If he made a kick at Blincoe, so great was his strength, it commonly lifted him off the floor. If he struck him, even a flat-handed blow, it floored him; If, with a stick, it not only bruised him, but cut his flesh. It was not enough to use his feet or his hands, but a stick, a bobby or a rope's-end. He and others used to throw rollers one after another, at the poor boy, aiming at his head, which, of course was uncovered while at work, and nothing delighted the savages more, than to see Blincoe stagger, and to see the blood gushing out in a stream! So far were such results from deterring the monsters, that long before one wound had healed, similar acts of cruelty produced others, so that, on many occasions, his head was excoriated and bruised to a degree, that rendered him offensive to himself and others, and so intolerably painful, as to deprive him of rest at night, however weary he might be. In consequence of such wounds, his head was over-run by vermin. Being reduced to this deplorable state, some brute of a quack doctor used to apply a pitch cap, or plaister to his head. After it had been on a given time, and when its adhesion was supposed to be complete, the *terrible doctor* used to lay forcibly hold of one corner and tear the whole scalp from off his head at once! This was the common remedy; I should not exaggerate the agonies it occasioned, were I to affirm, that it must be equal to any thing inflicted by the American savages, on helpless prisoners, with their scalping knives and tomahawks.

This same ruffian, (Robert Woodward) who, by the concurrent testimony of many sufferers, stands depicted, as possessing that innate love of cruelty which marked a Nero, a Caligula, or a Robespierre, used when Blincoe could not, or did not keep pace with the machinery, to tie him up by the wrists to a cross beam and keep him suspended over the machinery till his agony was extreme. To avoid the machinery, he had to draw up his legs every time it came out or returned. If he did not lift them up, he was cruelly beaten over the shins, which were bare; nor was he released, till growing black in the face, and his head falling over his shoulder, the wretch thought his victim was near expiring. Then after some gratuitous knocks and cuffs, he was released and instantly driven to his toil, and forced to commence, with every appearance of strength and vigour, though he were so much crippled, as to be scarcely able to stand. To lift the apprentices up by their ears, shake them violently, and then dash them down upon the floor with the utmost fury, was one of the many inhuman sports in Litton Mill, in which the overlookers appeared to take delight. Frequently has Blincoe been thus treated, till he thought his ears were torn from his head, and this for very trivial offences, or omissions. Another of these diabolical amusements consisted in filing the apprentices' teeth! Blincoe was once constrained to open his mouth to receive this punishment, and Robert Woodward applied the file with great vigour! Having punished him as much as he pleased; the brute said with a sneer; "I do this to sharpen thy teeth, that thou may'st eat thy Sunday dinner the better."

Blincoe declared, that he had often been compelled, on a cold winter's day, to work *naked*, except his trousers, and loaded with two half hundred weights slung behind him, hanging one at each shoulder. Under this cruel torture, he soon sunk; when, to make the sport last the longer, Woodward substituted quarter of hundred weights, and thus loaded, by every painful effort, Blincoe could not lift his arm to the roller. Woodward has forced him to wear these weights for hours together, and still to continue at his work! Sometimes, he has been commanded to pull off his shirt and get into a large square skip, when, the savage, being sure of his mark, and that, not a blow would be lost, used to beat him till he was tired! At other times, Blincoe has been hoisted upon other boys' shoulders, and beaten with sticks till he has been shockingly discoloured and covered with contusions and wounds.

What spinners call, a *draw off*, at one of those frames at which Blincoe worked, required about forty seconds. Woodward has often insisted upon Blincoe cleaning all the cotton away under the whole frame, in a single draw, and to go out at the further end, under pain of a severe beating. On one of these occasions, Blincoe had nearly lost his life, being caught between the faller and the head piece, his head was jammed between them. Both his temples were cut open and the blood poured down each side of his face, the marks to be seen! It was considered next to a miracle, that he escaped with his life! So far from feeling the least compassion, Woodward beat him cruelly, because he had not made *more haste*! Blincoe says, to the best of his recollection, he was twelve years of age, when this accident happened.

It is a fact, too notorious to be denied, that the most brutal and ferocious of the spinners, stretchers, rovers, &c. have been in the habit, from mere wantonness, of inflicting severe punishments upon piecers, scavengers, frame-tenters, winders, and others of the juvenile class, subjected to their power, compelling them to eat dirty pieces of candle, to lick up tobacco spittle, to open their mouths for the filthy wretches to spit into; all which beastialities have been practised upon the apprentices at Litton Mill! Among the rest, Blincoe has often suffered these indignities. What has a tendency to display human nature in its worst state, is, that most of the overlookers, who acted thus cruelly, had arrived in the mill as parish apprentices, and, as such, had undergone all these offensive inflictions!

There was, however, one diversion, which, in all my enquiries as to cotton-mill *amusements*, I never found parallelled. Of this Robert

Woodward, if I mistake not, has a claim to the honour of being the *original inventor*. It was thus executed.—A tin can or cylinder, about three feet high, to receive the rovings, and about nine or ten inches in diameter, was placed in the midst of the alley or wheel-house, as the space is called, over which the frames travel at every draw, and pretty close to the race. Upon this can or hollow cylinder, Blincoe had to mount; and there to stand upon one foot, holding a long brush extended in the opposite hand, until the frame came out, about three times in two minutes, invariably knocking the can from under him, both fell to the floor. The villian used to place the can so near the race, that there was considerable danger of Blincoe falling on it, and, if so, it would probably have lamed him for life if it had not killed him on the spot; and he had, with the utmost possible celerity, to throw himself flat upon the floor, that the frame might pass over him! During this short interval, the amateurs, i.e. Robert Woodward, Charnock, Merrick, &c. used to set the can upright again, and it required no small share of ingenuity, in them, to keep time. The frame being returned, poor Blincoe had to leap on his feet, and again to mount nimbly on the hollow column of tin, again to extend his arm, holding the long hair brush, and again sustain a fall, amidst the shouts and yells of these fiends. Thus would the villians continue to persecute and torment him, till they were tired, notwithstanding the *sport* might have been his death. He ran the risk of a broken bone, or the dislocation of a limb, every time he was thus thrown down; and the time the monsters thus wasted, they afterwards made up by additional labour wrung from their wretched victims!

Another of their diversions consisted in tying Blincoe's hands behind him and one of his legs up to his hands. He had then only one leg left free to hop upon, and no use left of his hands to guard him, if he chanced to fall, and if Blincoe did not move with activity, the overlooker would strike a blow with his clenched fist, or cut his head open by flinging rollers. If he fell, he was liable to have his leg or arm broken dislocated. Every one conversant with cotton-spinning machinery knows the danger of such *diversions*, and of their cruelty, every one can judge.

There seemed to exist a spirit of emulation, and infernal spirit, it might with justice be designated, among the overlookers of Litton Mill, of inventing and inflicting the most novel and singular punishments. For the sake of being the better able, and more effectually to torment their victims, the overlookers allowed their thumb and fore-finger nails to grow to an extreme length, in order that, when they *pinched their ears*, they might make their nails meet, *marks to be seen*.

Needham himself the owner of the Mill, stands arraigned of having the cruelty to act thus, very frequently, till their blood ran down their necks, and so common was the sport, it was scarcely noticed. As regarded Blincoe, one set of wounds had not seldom time to heal, before another set was inflicted; the general remedy that Blincoe applied was, the oil used to keep the machinery in order. The despicable wretches, who thus revelled in acts of lawless oppression, would often, to indulge the whim of a moment, fling a roller at a boy's head, and inflict deep wounds, and this, frequently, without even a shadow of a fault to allege, or even a plausible reason to assign in justification! At another time, if the apprentices stood fair for the infliction of a stripe, with a twig or the whip, the overlookers would apply it, with the utmost vigour, and then, bursting into laughter, call it a —— *good hit*! Blincoe declared he had, times innumerable been thus assailed, and has had his head cut severely, without daring to complain of the cause. Woodward and others of the overlookers used to beat him with pieces of the thick leathern straps made supple by oil, and having an iron buckle at the end, which drew blood almost every time it was applied, or caused severe contusions.

Among Blincoe's comrades in affliction, was an orphan boy, who came from St. Pancras workhouse, whose proper name was James Nottingham; but better known as "*blackey*," a nick name that was given to him, on account of his black hair, eyes, and complexion. According to Blincoe's testimony, this poor boy suffered even greater cruelties, than fell to his own share! by an innumerable number of blows, chiefly inflicted on his head!—by wounds and contusions, his head swelled enormously, and he became stupid! To use Blincoe's significant expression, "his head was as soft as a boiled turnip," the scalp on the crown, pitting every where on the least compression. This poor boy, being reduced to this most pitiable condition, by unrestrained cruelty, was exposed to innumerable outrages, and was, at last, incapable of work, and often plundered of his food!—melancholy and weeping, he used to creep into holes and corners, to avoid his tormentors. From mere debility, he was inflicted by incontinency of stools and urine! To punish this infirmity, conformably as Blincoe declared, to the will of Ellice Needham, the master, his allowance of broth, butter-milk, porridge, &c. was withheld! During the summer time, he was mercilessly scourged! In winter, stripped quite naked, and he was slung, with a rope tied round his shoulders, into the dam, and dragged to and fro, till he was nearly suffocated. They would then draw him out, and sit him on a stone, under a pump, and pump upon his head, in a copious stream, while some stout fellow was employed to sluice the poor wretch with pails of water, flung with all possible fury into his face. According to the account I received, not alone Blincoe, but several other of the Litton Mill apprentices, when these horrid inflictions had reduced the poor boy to a state of idiotism,—his wrongs and sufferings,—his dismal condition,—far, from exciting sympathy, but increased the mirth of these vulgar tyrants! His wasted and debilitated frame was seldom, if ever, free from wounds and contusions, and his head covered with running sores and swarming with lice, exhibited a loathsome object! In consequence of this miserable state of filth and disease, poor Nottingham has many times had to endure the excruciating torture of the pitch and scalping cap already named!

Having learnt, in 1822, that this forlorn child of misery was then at work in a cotton factory, near Oldfield Lane, I went in search of and found him. At first, he seemed much embarrassed, and when I made enquiries as to his treatment at Litton Mill, to my surprise, he told me "he knew nothing whatever about it." I then, related what Blincoe and others had named to me, of the horrid tortures he endured. "I dare say," said he mildly, "he told you truth, but I have no distinct recollection of any thing that happened to me during the greater part of the time I was there! I believe," said he, "my sufferings was most dreadful, and that I nearly lost my senses." From his appearance, I guessed he had not been so severely worked as others of the poor crippled children whom I had seen! As well as I can recollect, his knees were not deformed, or if at all, but very little! He is much below the middle size, as to stature. His

55

countenance round, and his small and regular features, bore the character of former sufferings and present tranquility of mind.

In the course of my enquiries respecting this young man, I was much gratified, by hearing the excellent character given him in the vicinity of his lodging. Several persons spoke of him as being serious and well inclined, and his life and conduct irreproachable.

We frequently had our best dinner in the week on a Sunday, and it was generally broth, meat and turnips, with a little oat-cake, the meat was of as coarse a sort as could be bought. This being our extra dinner, we did not wish to part with it too soon, therefore it was a general practice amongst the 'prentices to save some of it until Monday, in the care of the governor of the 'prentice-house, and for each one to know their own. The practice was to cut in their oat-cake, some mark or other, and lay it on their wooden trenchers. It happened one Sunday we had our dinner of bacon broth and turnips with a little oat-cake. This Sunday, one Thomas Linsey, a fellow 'prentice thought he could like a snack, early in the morning, therefore he took a slice of bacon between two pieces of oat-cake to bed with him, and put it under his head I cannot say, under his pillow, because we never was allowed any. The next morning about three or four o'clock, as it was a usual practice in the summer time when short of water, for a part of the hands to begin their work sooner, by this contrivance we was able to work our full time or near. Linsey was found dead in bed, and as soon as some of the 'prentices knew of his death, as they slept about 50 in a room, there was a great scuffle who should have the bacon and oat-cake from under his head, some began to search his pockets for his tin, this tin he used to eat his victuals with; some had pieces of broken pots, as no spoons was allowed. It was reported this Sunday that this pig had died in the Lees, a place so called at the back of the 'prentice-house. There was no coroner's inquest held over Linsey to know the cause of his death. I shall leave the reader to judge for himself this distressing sight, at so early an hour in the morning.—This occurred at Litton Mill.

It might be supposed, that these horrid inflictions had been practised, in this cotton-factory, unknown to the master and proprietor of Litton Mill; but the testimony, not of Blincoe alone, but of many of his former associates unknown to him, gave similar statements, and like Blincoe, described Ellice Needham the master, as equalling the very worst of his servants in cruelty of heart! So far from having taken any care to stop their career, he used to animate them by his own example to inflict punishment in any and every way they pleased. Mr. Needham stands accused of having been in the habit of knocking down the apprentices with his clenched fists;—kicking them about when down, beating them to excess with sticks, or flogging them with horse-whips; of seizing them by they ears, lifting them from the ground and forcibly dashing them down on the floor, or pinching them till his nails met! Blincoe declares his oppressors used to seize him by the hair of his head and tear it off by a handful at a time, till the crown of his head had become as bald as the back of his hand! John Needham, following the example of his father, and possessing unlimited power over the apprentices, lies under the imputation of crimes of the blackest hue, exercised upon the wretched creatures, from whose laborious toil, the means of supporting the pomp and luxury in which he lived were drawn. To boys, he was a tyrant and an oppressor! To the girls the same, with the additional odium of treating them with an indecency as disgusting as his cruelty was terrific. Those unhappy creatures were at once the victims of his ferocity and his lust.

For some trivial offence, Robert Woodward once kicked and beat Robert Blincoe, till his body was covered with wheals and bruises. Being tired, or desirous of affording his young master the luxury of amusing himself on the same subject, he took Blincoe to the counting-house, and accused him of wilfully spoiling his work. Without waiting to hear what Blincoe might have to urge in his defence, young Needham eagerly looked about for a stick; not finding one at hand, he sent Woodward to an adjacent coppice, called the Twitchell, to cut a supply, and laughingly bade Blincoe strip naked, and prepare himself for a good *flanking*! Blincoe obeyed, but to his agreeable surprise, young Needham abstained from giving him the promised flanking. The fact was, the poor boy's body was so dreadfully discoloured and inflamed by contusions, its appearance terrified the young despot, and he spared him, thinking that mortification and death might ensue, if he laid on an other "flanking." Hence his unexpected order to Blincoe to put on his things! There was not, at the time, a free spot on which to inflict a blow! His ears were swollen and excoriated; his head, in the most deplorable state imaginable; many of the bruises on his body had suppurated! and so excessive was his soreness, he was forced to sleep on his face, if sleep he could obtain, in so wretched a condition!

Once a week, and generally after sixteen hours of incessant toil, the eldest girls had to comb the boys' heads; an operation, that being alike painful to the sufferer, as disgusting to the girls, was reluctantly endured, and inefficiently performed. Hence arose the frequency of scald-heads and the terrible scalping remedy! Upon an average, the children were kept to work during a great part, if not all, the time Blincoe was at Litton Mill, sixteen hours in the day. The result of this excessive toil, superadded to hunger and torture, and was the death of many of apprentices, and the entailment of incurable lameness and disease on many others.

The store pigs and the apprentices used to fare pretty much alike; but when the swine were hungry, they used to speak and grunt so loud, they obtained the wash first, to quiet them. The apprentices could be intimidated, and made to keep still. The fatting pigs fared luxuriously, compared with the apprentices! They were often regaled with meal-balls made into dough, and given in the shape of dumplings! Blincoe and others, who worked in a part of the Mill, whence they could see the swine served, used to say to one another—*The pigs are served; it will be our turn next.*" Blincoe and those who were in a part of the building contiguous to the pigsties, used to keep a sharp eye upon the fatting pigs, and their meal-balls, and, as soon as he saw the swine-herd withdraw, he used to slip down stairs, and, stealing slyly towards the trough, plunge his hand in at the loop holes, and steal as many dumplings as he could grasp! The food thus obtained from a pigs trough, and, perhaps, defiled by their filthy chops, was exultingly conveyed to the privy or the duck-hole, and there devoured with a much keener appetite, than it would have been by the pigs; but the pigs, though generally esteemed the most stupid of animals, soon hit upon an expedient, that baffled the hungry boys; for the instant the meal-balls were put into their troughs, they voraciously seized them, threw them into the dirt, out of the reach of the boys! Not this alone; but, made wise by repeated losses, they kept a sharp look out, and the moment they ascertained the approach of the half-famished apprentices, they set up so loud a chorus of snorts and grunts, it was heard in the kitchen, when out rushed the swine-herd, armed with a whip, from which combined means of protection for the swine, this accidental source of obtaining a *good dinner* was soon lost! Such was the contest carried on for a time at Litton Mill, between the half-famished apprentices, and the well-fed swine.

I observed to Blincoe, it was not very rational, to rob the pigs, when they were destined to bleed to supply them with food, as soon as they grew sufficiently fat! "Oh! you're mistaken," said he, "these pigs were fatted for master's own table, or were sold at Buxton! We were fed upon the very worst and cheapest of Irish-fed bacon." There was, it seems, a small dairy at Litton Mill; but the butter was all sent to his house. The butter-milk alone was dispensed, and but very scantily, to the apprentices. About a table-spoonful of meal was distributed once a week to the apprentices, with which to wash themselves, instead of soap; but in nine cases out of ten, it was greedily devoured, and a piece of clay or sand, or some such thing, substituted: such was the dreadful state of hunger in which these poor children were kept in this mill.

To attempt a specific statement, how often Blincoe has been kept to work from five in the morning till midnight, during his period of servitude, would be hazardous! According to his own testimony, supported by that of many others, it was, at times of common occurrence, more especially on the Saturday! In most mills, the adult spinners left off on that day at *four* in the afternoon, whilst in these, where parish apprentices were employed, it was often continued, not only till midnight; but till six o'clock on the Sunday morning!

Exertion so incessant could not fail to reduce the majority of apprentices to a state of exhaustion and lassitude, so great as nearly to disqualify them to benefit by such instructions as an illiterate clown could afford, who officiated on Sundays as schoolmasters, or by divine worship, when they were allowed to attend. Nothing could be more cheerless, than the aspect of these juvenile sufferers, these helpless outcasts, nor more piteous than the wailings and lamentations of that portion, chiefly of the tenderest years, whom long familiarity with vice and misery had not rendered wholly callous.

A blacksmith or mechanic, named William Palfrey, who resided at Litton, worked in a room under that where Blincoe was employed. He used to be much disturbed by the shrieks and cries of the boys, whom the manager and overlookers were almost continually punishing. According to Blincoe's declaration, and that of others, human blood has often run from an upper to a lower floor, shed by these merciless task-masters. Unable to bear the shrieks of the children, Palfrey used to knock against the floor, so violently, as to force the boards up, and call out "for shame! for shame! are you murdering the children?" He spoke to Mr. Needham, and said, he would not stay in the mill, if such doings were allowed. By this sort of conduct, the humane blacksmith was a check on the cruelty of the brutal overlookers, as long as he continued in his shop; but he went away home at seven o'clock, and as soon as Woodward, Merrick, and Charnock knew that Palfrey was gone, they used to pay off the day's score, and to beat and knock the apprentices about without moderation or provocation, giving them black eyes, broken heads; saying, "I'll let you know old Palfrey is not here now!" To protract the evil hour, the boys, when they used to go down stairs for rovings, would come back and say—"Palfrey and the joiner are going to work all night," and sometimes by this manœuvre, they have escaped punishment.

It happened one day, when Blincoe was about twelve years old, he went to the counting-house with a cop, such being the custom at every doffing. While Blincoe was there, another apprentice, named Isaac Moss, came in on the same errand. Upon the floor stood the tin treacle can, with about 14 pounds of treacle. The sight arrested the attention of Blincoe, who said softly, "Moss, there is the treacle can come from Tideswell!"—"Eh," Moss exclaimed, "so it is." Blincoe said, "I have no spoon." Moss rejoined, "I have two." Putting his hand to his bosom and pulling out the bowl of an iron spoon and another which he kept for another person, down they sat on the floor opposite to each other, with the can between them and began operations, lading away as fast as they could! Blincoe had a large sized mouth, and in good condition, but the ruffian, William Woodward the manager, brother to Robert Woodward, having struck Moss a severe blow on the mouth, with a large stick, it had swollen so much, that the poor lad had the mortification of hardly being able to use it, and Blincoe could stow away at least three spoonsful to Moss's one! While the conscious pair were thus employed, the enemy, unheard and unperceived, stole upon them. It was a dark night; but there was a fire in the counting-house, by the light of which, over some glass above the top of the door, that grim spectre, the terror and the curse of these poor boys, Woodward, saw their diversion! He stood viewing them some time, when suddenly rushing upon them, he seized upon them as a cat pounces upon cheese-eating mice! Blincoe being most active with his feet, as well as with his spoon, after receiving a few kicks and cuffs, ran off to the factory, leaving Moss in the power, and at the mercy of William Woodward.

At ten o'clock the factory bell rang, and Blincoe went off to the apprentice-house, trembling with apprehension and looking wildly around amongst the apprentices, in hope of seeing his comrade Moss; but Moss was not to be seen! Presently, an order arrived from Woodward, for the master of the apprentices to bring down Blincoe! Richard Milner, the then governor of the apprentices, a corpulent old man, said, "Parson, what hast thou been doing?"— "Nothing," said the parson; his tremulous voice and shaking limbs contradicting his laconic reply; and away they trudged. When they got to the counting-house, they found Moss stuck erect in a corner, looking very poorly, his mouth and cheeks all over treacle. William Woodward, in a gruff voice, said, "So you have been helping to eat this treacle?"—"I have only eaten a little, Sir." Upon which, he hit Blincoe one of his flat-handed slaps, fetching fire from his eyes, and presently another, another, and another, till Blincoe began to vociferate for mercy, promising never to eat forbidden treacle any more! Woodward was full six feet high, with long arms, huge raw bones and immense sized hands, and when he had tired himself with beating Blincoe, he exclaimed: "Damn your bloods, you rascals, if you don't lap up the whole can of treacle,

I'll murder you on the spot." This denunciation was music to Blincoe's ears, who had never before received such an invitation. To accommodate the young gentlemen, the governor sent to his own kitchen for two long spoons, and then, with renewed execrations, Woodward bade them set to. Moss then crept softly and silently out of his corner, having been cruelly beaten in Blincoe's abscence! Looking ruefully at each other, down the culprits knelt a second time, one on each side of the treacle can! Blincoe had still the best of the sport; for poor Moss's mouth remained deprived of half its external dimensions, and being so excessively sore, he could hardly get in a tea-spoon, where Blincoe could shovel in large table-spoonsful! Moss kept fumbling at his lame mouth, and looking rather spitefully at Blincoe, as if he thought he would eat all the treacle. Meanwhile Milner and Woodward sat laughing and chatting by the fire side, often looking at the treacle-eaters, and anxiously waiting an outcry for quarters! Blincoe ate in a masterly style; but poor Moss could not acquit himself half as well, the treacle trickling down his chin, on both sides of his mouth, seeing which, Woodward suddenly roared out, "Damn you, you villian, if you don't open your mouth wider, I'll open it for you." Poor Moss trembled; but made no reply, and Blincoe being willing to make hay while the sun shone, instead of falling off, seemed, at every mouthful, to acquire fresh vigour! This surprised and mortified Woodward not a little, who seeing no signs of sickness, hearing no cry for quarter, and being apprehensive of an application for another can, got up to reconnoitre, and, to his amazement, found that the *little Parson*, who was not a vast deal higher than the can, had almost reached the bottom, and displayed no visible loss or diminution of appetite!

Inexpressibly vexed at being thus outwitted before the governor, he roared out in a tremendous voice to Milner, "Why damn their bloods, they'll eat the whole! Halt, you damned rascals, or, I'll kill you on the spot!" In a moment, Blincoe ceased his play, and licked his lips and spoon, to shew how keen his stomach still was! Milner and Woodward then took stock, and found, that, out of fourteen pounds, not three remained; Milner laughed immoderately at Woodward, to think what a luscious mode of punishment he had found out for treacle stealers!—Woodward being extremely exasperated, ordered Samuel Brickleton, an overlooker, to fasten

Moss and Blincoe together with handcuffs, of which as well as of *fetters*, there were plenty at Litton Mill, and then forced them to carry the can to the apprentice-house between them. When they arrived at the door, his hand being small, Blincoe contrived to withdraw it from the handcuff, and ran nimbly off into the room amongst the apprentices, leaving the treacle can in Moss's hand. Brickleton, unconscious of Blincoe's escape, arrived in the kitchen, where the Governor and his family resided, looked round, and seeing only one prisoner, cried out, "Eh! where's Parson gone." Moss said, he believed he was gone into the apprentice-house. Brickleton examined the handcuffs and finding they were locked, was much puzzled to think how the parson had contrived to get his hand out. The kind and careful Mrs. Milner, knowing there was money due to Blincoe, for working his dinner-hour, viz. a farthing a day, proposed to have it stopped, to pay for the treacle which Woodward had compelled him to eat, on pain of putting him instantly to death. Such was the law and equity, which prevailed at Litton Mill! That night, in consequence of his sumptuous supper, Blincoe was forbidden to enter his bed, and he laid all night, in the depth of winter, on the hard cold floor.

This part of the subject requires an explanation, as to the equivalent given by the owner to the apprentices, in lieu of their dinner hour. This hour consisted, in general, of forty minutes, and not always so many. The master, to induce the apprentices to work all day long, promised each three-pence per week, if they worked the whole of the dinner hour, and they had to eat it, *bite and sup*, at their work, without, spoon, knife, or fork, and with their dirty oily fingers! They were thus kept on their feet, from five o'clock in the morning, till nine, ten, and even eleven o'clock at night, and on Saturdays, sometimes till twelve; because Sunday was a *day of rest*! Frequently, though almost famishing, the apprentices could not find time to eat their food at all; but carried it back with them at night, covered with flue and filth. This liberality did not last long. The halfpenny was reduced to a farthing, and this farthing was withheld till it amounted to several shillings, and then, when the master *pleased*, he would give a shilling or two, and none dare ask for more. Those whom the overlookers pleased to order so to do, had to work their dinner hour for nothing, and their comrades used to fetch their dinners, who, not unfrequently, pilfered a part. The money thus earned, the poor 'prentices used to reserve, to buy wheaten cakes, and red herrings, to them, luxuries of the most delicious kind. Such was the miserable manner in which they were fed, that, when they gave the pence to Palfrey (the smith,) to bring the tempting cake of wheaten flour, and the herring, in the morning, they used to say to their comrades. "Old Palfrey is to bring me a cake and herring in the morning. Oh! how greedily I shall devour them." They commonly dreamt of these anticipated feasts, and talked of their expected luxuries in their sleep. When Palfrey arrived, they would, if they dared, have met him on the stairs, or have followed him to the smithy; but, in an eager whisper, enquired "have you brought my cake and herring?" "Aye, lad," said Palfrey, holding out the expected provisions. Eagerly they seized the herring and the cake, and the first full bite generally took off head or tail, as it came first to hand, while the cake was thrust inside their bosom; for they worked with their shirt collar open and generally without jackets. The poor souls, who, having no pence, could have no dainties, would try to snatch a piece slyly, if it were possible, and if that failed, they would try to beg a morsel. If the possessor gave a taste, he held the herring so tight, that only a very small portion could be bitten off, without biting off the ends of the owner's fingers, and their whole feast was quickly finished, without greatly diminishing their appetite. It happened, by some extraordinary stroke of good fortune, that Blincoe became possessed of a shilling, and he determined to have what he termed, a proper blow out; he, therefore, requested Palfrey to bring him six penny wheaten cakes, and half a pound of butter. Blincoe was then a stretcher, and had, as such, a better opportunity to receive and eat his dainties unobserved. The cakes he pulled one by one, from his bosom, and laying them upon the frame, spread the butter on them with a piece of flat iron, and giving his two comrades a small part each, he set to and devoured all the rest; but the unusual quantity and quality nearly made him ill. Blincoe had no appetite for his dinner or supper, and, he, therefore, let another comrade eat it, who engaged to give Blincoe his when he happened to lose his appetite. Such were the prospective and contingent negotiations carried on by these wretched children, relative to their miserable food.

If Blincoe happened to see any fresh cabbage leaves, potato or turnip parings, thrown out upon the dunghill, he has ran down with a can full of sweepings, as an excuse, and as he threw that dirt on the dunghill, he would eagerly pick the other up, and carry it in his shirt, or in his can, into the mill, wipe the dirt off as well as he could, and greedily eat them up. At other times, when they had rice puddings boiled in bags for dinner—the rice being very bad and full of large maggots, Blincoe not being able to endure such food, used to go into one of the woods near the factory, and get what the boys called *bread and cheese*, that is, hips and hipleaves, clover, or other vegetable, and filling his bosom, run back to the mill, and eat his trash, instead of fowl rice, with which neither butter-milk, milk, treacle, nor even a morsel of salt, was allowed.

Amongst the most singular punishments inflicted upon Blincoe, was that of screwing small hand-vices of a pound weight, more or less, to his nose and ears, one to each part; and these have been kept on, as he worked, for hours together! This was principally done by Robert Woodward, Merrick and Charnock. Of these petty despots, Merrick was the most unpardonable, as he had been a parish apprentice himself, and ought to have had more compassion. This Merrick was a stretcher, and Blincoe when about 11 or 12 years old, used to stretch for him, while he, Merrick, ate his dinner. Out of kindness, or because he could not eat it himself, Merrick used occasionally to leave a small part of his allowance, and tell Blincoe to go and eat it. On Mondays, it was the custom to give the boys bread and treacle, and turnip *broth* made the day before, which generally stunk to such a degree, that most of the poor creatures could only pick out the oat bread, the broth being loathsome. Whenever Merrick left a bit of bread and treacle in the window, Blincoe used to run eagerly at the prize, and devour it voraciously. On Monday, this overlooker, who was a most inhuman task-master, sent Blincoe down to the card-room for a basket of rovings, a descent of four or five stories deep, for this burthen of considerable weight. During the time he was gone, Merrick rubbed tar upon the oat cake, and laid it in the window as usual. When Blincoe returned, the brute said, "go and eat what lies in the window." Blincoe seeing as he supposed, so much treacle upon the bread, was surprised; for Merrick usually licked it clean off, and to his bitter mortification, found, instead of treacle, it was TAR. Unable to endure the nauseous mouthful, Blincoe spat it out, whilst Merrick, laughing at him, said, "What the devil are you spitting it out for." Poor Blincoe, shaking his head, said, "You know, mon," and Blincoe left the remainder of the tarred cake in the window, when his comrade, Bill Fletcher, a poor lad since dead, who came from Peak Forest, took up the bread, and scraping off the tar as clean as he could, ate it up, apparently with a good appetite! To such dreadful straits were they driven by hunger, the apprentices have been known to *pick turnips out of the necessary*, which others, who had stolen them, had thrown there to conceal, and washing them, have devoured the whole, thinking it too extravagant even to waste the peeling.

Palfrey, the Smith, had the task of rivetting irons upon any of the apprentices, whom the masters ordered, and those were much like the irons usually put upon felons! Even young women, if suspected of intending to run away, had irons riveted on their ancles, and reaching by long links and rings up to the hips, and in these they were compelled to walk to and from the mill to work and to sleep! Blincoe asserts, he has known many girls served in this manner. A handsome-looking girl about the age of twenty years, who came from the neighbourhood of Cromford, whose name was Phebe Rag, being driven to desperation by ill-treatment, took the opportunity, one dinner-time, when she was alone, and when she supposed no one saw her, to take off her shoes and throw herself into the dam, at the end of the bridge, next the apprentice-house. Some one passing along, and seeing a pair of shoes, stopped. The poor girl had sunk once, and just as she rose above the water he seized her by the hair! Blincoe thinks it was Thomas Fox, the governor, who succeeded Milner, who rescued her! She was nearly gone, and it was with some difficulty her life was saved! When Mr. Needham heard of this, and *being afraid the example might be contagious*, he ordered James Durant, a journeyman spinner, who had been apprenticed there, to take her away to her relations at Cromford, and thus she escaped!

When Blincoe's time of servitude was near expiring, he and three others, namely, William Haley, Thomas Gully, and John Emery, the overlookers, took a resolution, to go out of the factory, at a fixed hour, meaning not to work so many hours; but, according to Blincoe's account, neither he nor his comrades had ever heard up to that time, of any law which regulated the hours of apprentices working in cotton-mills, nor did they know what an act of parliament meant, so profound was the ignorance in which they had been reared! Blincoe and his mutinous comrades, having left work at the expiration of fourteen hours labour, went off to the apprentice-house. Upon this, the manager, William Woodward, sent off an express to the master, (Mr. Needham), at Highgate Wall, a lone and large mansion about four miles distant. Orders came back, to turn all four out of the apprentice-house that night; but not to give them any provisions! Being thus turned out, Blincoe got lodging with Samuel Brickleton! One or two of his comrades slept in the woods, which luckily was hay time.—Brickleton's hospitality did not include provisions, and having had no food since twelve o'clock the day before, Blincoe was sorely hungry in the morning, but still he had nought to eat! About nine o'clock, all four, agreeable to the orders they received the night before, went to the counting-house at the mill. Mr. Needham was there in a terrible ill-humour—As soon as he saw Blincoe come in, he took from his body, his waistcoat and jacket, and fell upon him with his thick walking-stick, which he quickly broke by the heavy blows laid on poor Blincoe's head and shoulders, and he kept on swearing the while, "*I'll run you out, you damned rascal.*" As soon as he could escape, Blincoe ran off to his work, when Haley and Emery, who were apprentices, like Blincoe, caught their share of his fury! At noon, Blincoe went eager enough to the apprentice house, having had no food for twenty-four hours. Having in a few minutes, devoured his portion, he ran off at full speed, without hat, jacket, or waistcoat, his head and body greatly bruised, towards the residence of a magistrate, named Thornelly, who resided at Stanton-Hall, a place about six miles beyond Bakewell, and eleven from Litton-Mill! There resided, at this time, at Ashford, about four miles from Litton-Mill, a man named Johnny Wild, a stocking-weaver, who had been his (Blincoe's) overlooker, when first he went to Lowdham Mill. Filled with the fond hope of being made at once a gentleman, thither, poor Blincoe, now twenty years of age, directed his course. Johnny Wild was sitting at his frame, weaving stockings, and was surprised to see Blincoe run up to the door like a wild creature, terror in his looks and reeking with perspiration, without hat, coat, or waistcoat. To him, Blincoe told the cruel usage he had met with, and the wounds and bruises he had just received, which were sufficiently visible! Wild and his wife seemed touched with compassion, at the sad plight Blincoe was in, gave him a bowl of bread and milk, lent him a hat, and directed him his way. Thus refreshed, the fugitive set off again, running as fast as he could, looking often behind him. As he passed through Bakewell, Blincoe thought it best to slacken his pace, lest some mercenary wretch, suspecting him to be a Litton Mill apprentice running away, should, in the hope of receiving a reward of a half-crown piece, seize him and send him back to prison! As he passed along many seemed to eye him intently; but no one stopped him. About six o'clock in the evening, being heartily jaded, he arrived at the house of Mr. Thornelly. It happened, that the magistrate was at dinner—but some person, in his employ, understanding that Blincoe came to seek redress for alleged violence, went to the supplicant in the yard, saying, "Who do you want?"—"Mr. Thornelly."—What for?—"I am an apprentice at Litton Mill, master has beat me cruelly, do look at my shirt?"— "Never mind, never mind," said this person, "you cannot see Mr. Thornelly to-day; he is at dinner; there will be a bench of justices to-morrow, about eleven in the morning, at the Sign of the Bull's Head, facing the church at Heam; you must go there." This place lay about five miles from Litton Mill, on the Sheffield road. Finding there was nothing to be done at Stanton-Hall, poor Blincoe began to measure back his weary stops to Litton Mill! He called at Johnny Wild's, as he returned, who allowed him to rest; but, of food, he could not offer any; having a large family, and being but a poor man, he had none to spare! Blincoe gave back his hat, and arrived at the apprentice-house between nine and ten, being then giving-over time! William Woodward, the manager, whose heavy hand had inflicted blows and cuffs beyond calculation on poor Blincoe, was about the first person by whom he was accosted! In a tone, about as gentle as that of a baited-bear, and an aspect much more savage, said, "Where have you been?"—"To Mr. Thornelly."—"I'll Thornelly you to-morrow," said he, and turned away. Not knowing what the next day might bring forth, Blincoe applied for his mess of water-porridge, which, after a journey of two and twenty miles, tasted highly savory, and then he retired to his bed, praying God to end his life, or mitigate its severity—a prayer that was common at Litton Mill!—Sore as he was, he slept; but it was on his face, his back being too much bruised, to lie in that position, or even on his side! In the morning, he rose and went to his stretching frame. Between seven and eight o'clock Blincoe saw Woodward going to the apprentice-house, from the window of the factory. Seeing this opportunity, without waiting for breakfast, Blincoe again made a start, still without hat, waistcoat or coat, towards Heam, to state to the magistrates the cruel treatment he had received—The day was fine. The hay was about, and miserable as was poor Blincoe, he could not but feel delighted with the sweet air and romantic scenery. Having been thus expeditious, Blincoe was at Heam, an hour and a half too soon. To amuse himself, he went into the Church-yard. As soon as the magistrates arrived, from whose hands he came to supplicate for justice, Blincoe went to the Bull's Head. The officiating clerk was an attorney named Cheek, who resided at Whetstone-Hall, a mansion situated within half a mile of Tideswell. To this person, Blincoe began unbosoming his grief, and in the earnestness of his harrangue, and fearful, lest the attorney did not catch every syllable, the half-naked Blincoe crept nearer and nearer; but Mr. Cheek not relishing the dense, foul scent of oil, grease, and filth, said, "Well, well, I can hear you, you need not come so near; stand back." Poor Blincoe, not a little mortified, obeyed his command, and, by the time Blincoe's piteous tale was ended, the magistrates had mostly arrived, to whom Mr. Cheek, the clerk to the magistrates, read the paper, which Blincoe supposed contained his intended deposition. Blincoe was then sworn. One of the magistrates, Blincoe believes it was a Mr. Middleton, of Leam Hall, said, "Where is Mr. Needham?"—Blincoe replied, "He's gone to-day (Tuesday) to Manchester Market." This prevented their sending a man and horse to fetch him. One of the magistrates then said to Blincoe, "Go strait to the mill, to your work."—"Oh! Sir, he'll leather me," meaning, Mr. Needham would beat him again. "Oh, no! he durst na'—he durst na'," said one of the magistrates in reply. Upon this, some one advised, that a letter should be sent to Mr. Needham, in whose much dreaded presence, Blincoe had no inclination to appear! Blincoe cannot recollect who wrote the letter, but thinks it was Mr. Middleton, who said, "If he leathers you, come to me." This gentleman resided at a distance of about eight miles from Litton Mill. Having this powerful talisman in his possession, Blincoe returned direct to the mill, and, advancing boldly to Woodward, the manager, said, "Here's a letter for Mr. John Needham," the son of the old master, who is now resident in Tideswell! Blincoe informed Woodward, he had been at a justice-meeting at Heam, and as a justice had sent this letter, Woodward did not dare to lay violent hands upon him. This day, poor Blincoe had to fast till night, making a complete round of another twenty-four hours of fasting! On Wednesday, John Needham returned from Manchester market, and appeared, as usual, at Litton Mill.—The letter, from which Blincoe anticipated such beneficial results, was handed to the young Squire, by William Woodward, the manager. He broke the seal, read it through, and ordered Blincoe to be called out of the factory, from his work. Obedient to the summons, and not a little alarmed, he appeared before his young master, whose savage looks shewed, ere he spoke a word, a savage purpose. The first words were, "Take off your shirt, you damned rascal!" Blincoe obeyed, his head and back being still very sore. John Needham instantly began flogging him with a heavy horse-whip, striking him with his utmost force, wherever he could get a blow. It was in vain Blincoe cried for quarters—in vain he promised never again to go to a Magistrate, in any case whatever. John Needham kept on flogging, swearing horribly and threatening furiously, resting between while, till he had fully satisfied his sense of justice! He then unlocked the door, and, saying, "You'll go again, will you?" bade Blincoe put on his shirt, and go to his work. Away went Blincoe, scarcely able to stand, and covered with additional bruises from head to foot. Even this horrid flogging did not deprive Blincoe of his appetite, nor of his determination to seek redress of the Magistrates, and accordingly, the next Sunday night, when some of the time-outs were let out of the prison, Blincoe, availing himself of the darkness of the night, watched the opening of the yard door, and crouching almost on his hands and knees, crept out unseen. Shortly after the order was given to set down to supper. Every 'prentice, male and female, knew their own places. In about two minutes, two hundred half-famished creatures were seated. Their names were called over, to see that none were missing, when, little parson could not be found. Governor Thomas Fox, on learning of this event, ordered the door warder to be called, who declared most vehemently, he had not let Blincoe out, and further, he had not passed the door; upon this, a general search was made in all the rooms and offices, high and low; but no where was little parson to be found. Meanwhile, as soon as Blincoe found himself outside the hated walls, he set off again up Slack, a very steep hill close to the mill, and made the best of his way to Litton, and going to the house of one Joseph Robinson, a joiner, who worked in Litton Mill, who had known Blincoe at Lowdham Mill, was well acquainted with the horrid cruelties he had suffered, and heartily compassionating Blincoe's miserable state, gave him a good supper, and let him sleep with his sons. In the morning, Robinson, who was really a humane man, and a friend to the poor children, gave Blincoe some bread and meat, and giving him a strict injunction not to own *where* he had slept. Blincoe set off, about six o'clock in the morning, to Mr. Middleton's house. The morning was showery, and Blincoe had neither hat, coat, or waistcoat, and he had about eight miles to go, in search of justice. He arrived at Mr. Middleton's long before his hour of appearance. At last, Mr. Middleton got up, and Blincoe approaching, crawling like a spaniel dog, said, "Sir, I have come again, Mr. Needham has been beating me worse than ever, as soon as he read your letter over." Seeing the miserable state Blincoe was in, drenched with the rain and half naked, Mr. Middleton said, "go into the kitchen and rest yourself— you should not have come here first; you should have gone to Mr. Cheek, of Whetstone Hall, and he would have given you a summons;" upon this, poor Blincoe said mournfully, "Eh, Sir, he will do nought for me—he is so thick with my master—they are often drinking together." "Pshaw, pshaw," said the Justice, "he's like to listen to you—he must;" but then, as if recollecting himself, he said, "Stop, I'll write you a letter to Mr. Cheek." In the Justice's kitchen, poor Blincoe got some bread and cheese, which was indeed a luxurious food, though unaccompanied with any beer. Blincoe thus refreshed, again set off to Mr. Cheek, a distance of about eleven or twelve miles, bareheaded and dressed only in trowsers and shoes. The rain continuing pouring in torrents. When Blincoe reached Whetstone Hall, one of the first persons he saw was a woman of the name of Sally Oldfield, her husband, Thomas Oldfield, then dead, had been governor of the 'prentices of Litton Mill. She was then housekeeper to Messrs. Shoro and Cheek, at Whetstone Hall. Those gentlemen were amongst the most intimate friends and visitors of Mr. Needham, and Sally Oldfield, who recollected Blincoe, alias parson, said, "Eh, Parson! what do you want here?" "I have a letter from Mr. Middleton to Mr. Cheek." "Eh!" said little old Sally again, "Are you going against your master?" Blincoe told her he was, and how cruelly he had been treated. Sally could not comprehend any right Blincoe had to complain, and said, "Eh! thou should'st not go against thy master." Saying this, she took him to the kitchen, gave him some bread and cheese, and plenty too, and some good beer, and then said, "Parson, thou must never go against thy master; what do you have for dinner on Monday?—do you have treacle now?" "No, we have dry bread and broth." "Ah," continued she, *Treacle is too dear.*" Blincoe could scarce refrain from smiling, recollecting the feast of the treacle can; but he said nothing, and not a soul came near him. There Blincoe sat until night, when he began to think the magistrates were hoaxing him, and he thought there was no utility in waiting for justice, or a possibility of obtaining redress! he would never more complain! seven hours sat Blincoe in Lawyer Cheek's kitchen, and not the least notice being taken of him or his letter, he made his solitary way back to the mill, and arrived there just as the mill had loosed, and going direct to Woodward, told him where he had been, and concealing the conviction he felt, that it not possible to obtain redress; he assured the tyrant, with tears and lamentations, that if he would intercede to prevent his being flogged again, he would never run away more. "On these conditions," said Woodward, "I will, if I can," and from that day Blincoe cannot recollect, that he was either flogged or beaten; but, *still* Blincoe had no knowledge, that there was any Act of Parliament for the protection of poor orphans like himself.—He knew of the magistrates coming to the mill; but he had no distinct idea that they came to *redress grievances*! So great was the terror of the poor ignorant apprentices, no one dared complain, and he cannot recollect that they ever gave themselves any other trouble, than merely going over the mill! Every thing was previously prepared and made ready. The worst of the cripples were put out of the way. The magistrates saw them not. The magistrates could never *find out* any thing wrong, nor hear of a single individual who had any complaint to make!—When Blincoe was about twelve or thirteen years of age, he well remembers an apprentice, almost grown up, who lost his life in an attempt to escape. He had tied several blankets or sheets together, to reach the ground from the chamber window, where he slept, which was three or four stories high. The line broke, he fell to the ground, and he was so much hurt at the fall, he died soon after. Blincoe thinks some surgeon or doctor came to him; but he has not the least recollection of any Coroner's inquest being held! In addition to the punishments already stated, Robert Woodward and other overlookers have kicked him down a whole flight of stairs; at other times, he has been seized by the hair of his head and dragged up and down the room, tearing off his hair by handsful, till he was almost bald! All the punishments he suffered, were inflicted upon others, and, in some cases, even to a worse degree than on himself. He even considers he came off tolerably well, compared with others, many of whom, he believes, in his conscience, lost their lives, and died at the apprentice-house, from the effects of hard usage, bad and scanty food, and excessive labour.

CHAPTER VI.

Blincoe remained in Litton Mill a year after he had received his indentures, not from inclination; but to get a little money to start with. His wages were only four shillings and sixpence weekly, and this was to have been paid monthly; but, month after month elapsed, and, instead of an honest settlement, there was nothing but shuffling! The first money he received was eighteen and sixpence, and being in possession of that sum, he thought himself incalculably rich! He scarcely knew what to do with it! It took away his appetite.—After he was a little composed, he devoted a few shillings to the purchase of some dainties, such as wheaten cakes and herrings! He then worked and lived like others, till his master owed him nearly half a years labour. The pay day came and then he drew nearly thirty shillings, the rest was kept back, so that Blincoe seeing no prospect before him but perpetual slavery for a merciless master, made up his mind to be off; and on Tidswell May fair, which happens on the fifteenth of May, he put his plan in execution! He knew not where to go; but started the next morning at hazard! When he came to Chapel-a-Frith, he determined to visit a celebrated fortune-teller, called Old Beckka'! She lived in a small back-house, a haggard, black, horrid-looking creature, very old, having a long beard, and dressed like a person who lived in ages past! Her name was very influential all over Derbyshire. So very famous was *old Beckka'*, that people came far and near, and she was reputed to be possessed of land and houses.—She never took a smaller fee than a shilling, even from the very poorest of her votaries. Her name was well-known at Litton Mill. If any thing was stolen, Woodward, the manager, or Gully, or some one of the overlookers, used to go to Chapel-a-Frith, to consult *old Beckka'*. To this sybil, Blincoe repaired, holding a shilling, between his thumb and finger! Perfectly understanding the object of his visit, she first took the shilling, and then said, "Sit down." He felt really frightened, and, if she had bade him stand upon his head, he declared he should have obeyed! He had been told, that she had really enchanted or bewitched persons, who had endeavoured to cheat or deceive her, or by whom she had been offended, causing them to lose their way, and sent ill fortune in many shapes. Our novice was also told, that ladies and gentlemen of high estate had come in their coaches, all the way from London, to learn their destiny, all which circumstances produced, on his uncultivated mind, the sensations described! No sooner was Robert Blincoe seated, than the witch of Chapel-a-Frith, put a common tea-cup in his hand, containing a little tea grounds, "Shake it well," said Beckka', Blincoe obeyed. Then the oracle drained away the water, and twirling the cup round and round, she affected, with the utmost gravity, to read his future fortune, in the figures described in the sediment at the bottom. Assuming a wild stare, and standing erect over him, her eyes apparently ready to leap from their sockets, she exclaimed, in a hollow sepulchral tone of voice, "You came from the outside of London, did you not?" "Yea," said the astonished Blincoe, "I did." "You came down in a waggon, and have been at a place surrounded with high rocks and great waters, and you have been used worse than a stumbling stone." Blincoe's mouth, and eyes, and ears, all seemed to open together, at this oracular speech, as he said, "Yea, yea, it is true." Then she said,—"Your troubles are at an end.—You shall rise above those, who have cast you down so low.—You shall see their downfall, and your head shall be higher than theirs.—Poor lad! terrible have been thy sufferings.—Thou shall get up in the world! you'll go to another place, where there'll be a big water, and so go thy way in peace, and may God prosper thy steps!" Filled with amazement, mingled with rising hopes of better fortune, Blincoe arose and departed, making a very low reverence to *"old Beckka'*," as he went out, and impressed with the fullest conviction, that she was truely a sorceress; the simpleton, forgetting, that his *costume*, his wild and pallid looks, and the *scent* of his garments, tainted as they were with the perfume of a cotton factory, were more than sufficient to point out to the fortune-teller, the past and present, from which she speedily fabricated the future fortune, for her simple visitor! Blincoe thought he got but a very short story for his shilling! On the other hand, he was very well contented with its *quality*, since it promised him, and in such positive terms, that he should rise above his cruel oppressor and become a great man. Filled with these thoughts, he stepped briskly along, not much encumbered with luggage; for he carried all his wardrobe on his back. When he arrived at a spot called "Orange end," where four ways met, he was perplexed which to take, the oracle of Chapel-a-Frith not having apprised him of this dilemma, nor which road to take! Being quite in an oracular mood, very happy, that he had got so far away from Litton, and fully convinced, that, go where he would, and befall him what would, he could not blunder upon a worse place, nor be oppressed by a more evil fortune, he tossed up a halfpenny in the air, making it spin round its own axis, and waiting its course as it rolled, resolved to follow in that direction. Its course happening to be pointed towards New Mills, Derbyshire, thither he bent his course, but failed in his application for work. Blincoe, therefore, walked on, till he came to Mr. Oldknow's Cotton Factory, at Mellow, and there he crept towards the counting-house, in an humble mood, and said, in a very meek tone of voice, "If you please, Sir, can you give me work?" The manager, Mr. Clayton, a gentleman by no means deficient in self-respect, asked sharply: "Where do you come from?" "From Litton Mill, Sir." "Where are your indentures?" "There they are, Sir," said Blincoe, holding up the papers. There were two or three gentlemen, in the counting-house, and they looked earnestly over the indentures and then at Blincoe, one of them saying, "Did you come from Pancras workhouse?" "Yes, Sir." "Why, we are all come from thence! we brought many children the other day to this Mill." "Indeed, Sir," said Blincoe, pitying, in his heart, the poor creatures, and thinking it would have been merciful to have killed them outright at once, rather than put them to such a place as Litton Mill had proved to him. Looking at the names of the subscribing officers and overseers, one of the Pancras parish officers said to Mr. Clayton: "Some of these officers are dead." Blincoe again exclaimed "Indeed, Sir,"—recollecting the atrocious lies and cruel deceptions, those men had practised upon him, in his infant years, by telling him to believe that, in sending him to a cotton-factory, he was to be made at once a gentleman; to live upon roast beef and plum-pudding; to ride his master's horses; to have a watch in his pocket and plenty of money, and nothing whatever to do! Poor Blincoe could not help thinking to himself:—"Where are the souls of these men gone, who, knowing the utter falsehood of their seductive tales, betrayed me to destiny far more cruel than transportation?" The overseers, looking at the distorted limbs of this victim of parochial economy, said "Why, how came you so lame? you were not so when you left London, were you?" "No, Sir, I was turned over, with the rest of the unclaimed 'prentices, from Lowdham Mill, to Ellice Needham, of Litton Mill." "How did they keep you?—what did you live upon?" "Water porridge—sometimes once, sometimes twice a day—sometimes potatoes and salt for supper: not half enough, and very bad food." "How many hours did you work?" "From five, or occasionally six o'clock in the morning, till nine, half-past ten, and sometimes eleven, and, on Saturday nights, till twelve o'clock." The person wrote these answers down; but made no comment, nor ever noticed the material facts; that Blincoe had not been taught the trade he should have learnt, and that the parish officers of Pancras had utterly neglected him and his miserable comrades, when the Lowdham Mill factory stopped! The manager then bade a person shew Blincoe where he might get lodgings, and bade him come to work in the morning. Blincoe was too much afraid of giving offence, by asking questions in the counting-house, to venture to enquire as to his parentage; but, as soon as he had got lodgings, he strove to make out where the officers were to lodge that night, at Mellor, to enquire further; but hearing they were just then gone, he was deprived of the opportunity! This occurrence, filling his mind with melancholy reflections, he shed many tears in solitude that night! The next morning, he went to his work, and found it was as hard as at Litton Mill; but of more moderate duration—the hours being from six in the morning, till seven in the evening. The 'prentices, whom he saw at work, seemed cheerful and contented—looked healthy and well, compared with those at Litton! They were well fed, with good milk-porridge and wheaten bread for breakfast, and all their meals were good and sufficient! They were kept clean, decently dressed, and every Sunday went twice to Marple Church, with Mr. Clayton, their under-master, at their head! On the whole, it struck Blincoe, that the children were in a Paradise, compared with the unfortunate wretches whom he had left at Litton Mill, and he indulged in the humane hope, that the lot of children just then brought down from London, might escape the dreadful sufferings he had had to endure! Unfortunately, the trade, which Blincoe had been fourteen or fifteen years articled to learn, was by no means so good as husbandry labour. The wages, Mr. Oldknow offered him, were *eleven shillings per week*, at the time that a good husbandry labourer could earn from sixteen shillings to a pound! After having been some months in Mr. Oldknow's factory, Blincoe learnt, that, whilst he did as much work, and as well as any man in the factory, which employed several hundred apprentices, Mr. Clayton had fixed his wages at three or four shillings per week less than any other person's. Blincoe could not impute this to any other cause, than an idea, that he was in so crippled a state, he dared not demand the same as another! Such is the mean and sordid spirit, that sways almost the whole of those establishments. When a poor creature has been crippled at one mill, and applies for work at another, instead of commiserating his condition and giving him the easiest and best work and best pay, it is a common custom, to treat them with the utmost contempt, and though they may be able to do their work as well for their masters, though not with the same ease to themselves, as one who has escaped being crippled, the masters generally make it a rule to screw them down to the very lowest point of depression, and, in many cases, give them only half their wages. On this principle was Blincoe dealt with at Mellor Factory; but, as the wretched diet on which he had been fed at Litton, enabled him to live upon three shillings per week, he saved money each week. Having an independent spirit and not being willing to work for less than his brethren, he took an opportunity one evening, to go to the counting-house and doffing his hat to Mr. Clayton, said, "Sir, if you please, will you be so good to rise my wages?" Turning sharp round, he said, "Raise your wages! why, I took you in upon *charity only*!" "I am sure it was very good of you, Sir," said Blincoe, who well knew that such hands as himself were scarce, therefore, that his charity began at home.—Hearing Blincoe speak in such humble, yet somewhat ironical terms; for he possessed a rich vein of sarcastic humour, Mr. Clayton said, "Well, go to your work, I'll see." They paid every fortnight at the factory.—The next pay night, Blincoe found himself paid at the rate of thirteen shillings, which was still two shillings under the price of other workmen! This continued a few weeks, when, an old servant, whom they had employed many years, applied for work, and on the Friday night fortnight, Blincoe's wages were sent up to him, with an order *to depart*. This is what is called *getting the bag*. Blincoe being alike surprised and hurt, and knowing he had done his work well and had never lost a minute, set an enquiry on foot, and he was told, from very good authority, it was because he had applied for an advance of wages, and because Mr. Clayton thought it was taking an advantage of him. Curious logic! Mr. Clayton seems totally to forget the advantage he had, in the first instance, taken of poor Blincoe, and feeling very sore, when the young fellow applied for redress, he seized this opportunity, and, in this petty way, to wreak his anger; and as the factory of Mr. Oldknow stood so very high, if compared with that of Ellice Needham, of Litton, these blemishes fully prove, how foul and corrupted is the spirit of traffic, since, in its best shape, it could not resist the temptation of taking a mean advantage of the necessities and the misery of a fellow creature.

Although the treatment of parish pauper apprentices was very liberal, compared to what they had endured at Litton Mill, the journeymen were governed by a very tight hand. If they arrived only two or three minutes after the clock had struck, they were locked out; and those, who were within, were all locked in, till dinner time, and not only were the outward doors, below, locked; but every room above, and there was a door-keeper kept, whose duty it was, a few minutes before the respective hours of departure, to unlock the doors, by whom they were again locked, as soon as the work-people arrived! In every door, there was a small aperture, big enough to let a quart can through, so that the food brought by parents and relations could be handed to them within—no one being permitted to go in or out, and, of course, the necessaries, two or three to each room, were within side the room, where the people worked! Such was the rigid order and severe discipline of one of the most *lenient* master cotton-spinners! Mr. Oldknow caused a road to be made from the turnpike to his mill, which saved some length of way, and every stranger, or person not absolutely working in the mill, who used it, had to pay a halfpenny—and, as the road led to New Mills and Mellor, those work-people, in common with all others, had to pay a halfpenny. There was a toll-house erected, and also a toll-bar, and the speculation, if not very neighbourly, is said to have been very profitable.

When Blincoe left this establishment, which seemed to vie with some of the largest factories in Manchester, both in its exterior grandeur, and in magnitude, he had contrived to save the greater part of his wages, and having a few pounds in his pocket, he felt less dismay at this harsh and unexpected treatment, than if he had acted with less prudence and been destitute. He had served faithfully and diligently upwards of half-a-year, and a character from so respectable an employer might be serviceable, he, therefore, made his appearance once more before Mr. Clayton, and doffing his hat, and assuming the most lowly and respectful attitude, said, in his usual slow and plaintive tone:—"Will you please, Sir, give me a character?"—"O no! O no!" replied the manager, "we never give characters here," with an unfriendly aspect! Blincoe thought it was better to be off and seek his fortune elsewhere, than stop and argue. This circumstance strongly marks the oppressive character of these establishments. It is clear, that Mr. Clayton did not chuse to hire Blincoe without a character, or something equivalent, by requiring to see his indentures; and, after the young man had served them diligently and honestly, for six months, he surely should have written to certify, that he had done so, and the denial *might* have prevented his getting another employer. However the law might stand at present, upon this point, in any future legislative measure, a clause should be introduced, to *compel* every master to give a written character, except where some positive act of gross misconduct interposed to neutralise the claim!

From Mellor Mill, Blincoe walked to Bollington, in Cheshire, a village not far from Macclesfield, and about 18 miles distance, having a bundle, which, slung upon a stick, he carried upon his shoulder. He passed several road-side houses of entertainment, allaying his thirst from the living fountains, and satisfying his hunger with a penny cake. In this way, he travelled, till he arrived at Bollington, where he obtained work in a factory, situated on the

Macclesfield road, belonging to a Mr. Lomax. He was placed in the card-room, which is reckoned the most laborious and unwholesome in the factory, on account of the great quantity of dirt and dust; but Mr. Lomax promised him a stretching frame, at the end of a fortnight. The fortnight having expired, Blincoe saw no signs of being relieved from stripping off the cotton from the cards. He made up his mind to be off, and march on towards Staley Bridge, in the hope of bettering his condition! As he was going along some fields, for a short cut, he was met by a couple of suspicious looking fellows, who, stepping boldly up to Blincoe, said in a stern voice, "What have you got in that bundle?" "I dunna know, Mester, but if you'll ask the gentleman on horseback, that is coming on the horse road, at the other side of the hedge, he'll tell you." Hearing this, and marking the calm indifference of Blincoe, the interrogators took to their heels, and never once looked behind them, as he could perceive; and thus the poor little wanderer outwitted the marauders, and saved his shirt and stockings, and, by the possibility, the hard-earned treasure he had in his fob. Having thus adroitly got rid of the thieves, Blincoe made the best of his way to the main road, and the best use of his legs, till he got in view of some houses, where he thought himself out of danger. Arrived at Staley Bridge, situate upon a river, which separates Cheshire and Lancashire, and where there are many spinning factories, he applied to a man named William Gamble, who had lived in Yorkshire. This man, twelve or thirteen years before, was one of the overlookers at Lowdham Mill, and very much addicting himself to kicking the apprentices and dragging them about by the hair of the head, up and down the rooms, and then dashing them upon the floor, on account of which propensity, he was reprimanded and removed, when the overseers of Pancras parish arrived. Indeed this man and one Smith, were the terror of the poor children; but Blincoe wanting work and knowing he was an overlooker in Mr. Harrison's factory, which, by way of pre-eminence, was called *the Bastile*, poor Blincoe had been so many years accustomed to Bastiles, he was not easily daunted. To Gamble he repaired, and who having bestowed so many marks of his *paternal* regard upon Blincoe, he recognized him at once and very kindly got him work at ten shillings per week, which he drew for the *use* of Blincoe, during a few weeks, to whom he acted as *caterer*, and provided him with a bed, so that Blincoe had nothing whatever to do, but his work, which was tolerably moderate, that is, compared with Litton Mill. Notwithstanding its unseemly appellative, the work-people were not locked up in the rooms, as at Mellor.

The master had another method of restraining his work people from going out, and which saved the pay of a door-keeper, namely, by the counting-house being so placed, the people could not go in or out without being seen! There Blincoe worked some months; but not being perfectly satisfied with the conditions in which the stewardship of William Gamble left him, he took the liberty to remove from his hospitable roof, and the result was, he could live upon and lay up one half of his wages. The wages paid at this mill were very low, and the work very laborious, being the stripping of the top cards! The fixed quantum was six pounds per day, which is a severe task. After this, the master went up to Blincoe and others, as they were at work, and informed them, he would have more weight of cotton stripped off the top cards, or turn them away, and Blincoe not feeling inclined to perform more work for that pay, asked for his wages and left the Bastile!

Hence, Blincoe went to Mr. Leech, the owner of another factory, at Staley Bridge, by whom he was engaged at nine shillings a week; but he found the cotton so foul and dirty, and the work so hard, he staid not long; as the owner paid only once in three weeks, it required some privation, before any wages could be got! After three days toil, Blincoe went to his master and asked him to lend as much silver as his work came to, and, having obtained it, he took French leave, to the great offence of his employer. Blincoe still remained at Staley Bridge, though unemployed. He next obtained work at the mill of a Mr. Bailey, whose father had then recently had one of his arms torn off by the blower, and he died in a few hours from the dreadful effects of that accident. Here Blincoe stopped, stripping of cards, for eleven shillings per week, during several months, when, having saved a few pounds, he determined to try his fortune at Manchester, which celebrated town was only seven or eight miles distant. Of London, Blincoe retained only a faint recollection, and he thought Manchester the largest and the grandest place in all the world. He took lodgings in St. George's-road, being attracted by the residence of James Cooper, a parish apprentice from the same workhouse with himself, who had been so cruelly flogged at Litton Mill. By this young man, Blincoe was received in a friendly manner, and he lodged in his house near Shudehill. Blincoe arrived at Manchester at a bad time, just at the return of peace, and he had a difficulty of getting work. His first place was in the factory of Mr. Adam Murray. There the engines worked only four days and a half per week; for which he received no more than seven shillings and a penny. Blincoe suffered much from the heat of the factories at Staley; but in this of Mr. Murray's, he found it almost suffocating, and if there had been as great a heat in the factory at Litton, added to the effects of long hours, and bad and scanty food, it is probably it had cut him off in the first year of his servitude! Blincoe, thinking it was wise to risk the chance of bettering his fortune, left Adam Murray's gigantic factory, at the end of the week, and next went to work in Robinson's factory,[1] as it is called, which belongs to Mr. Marriet. There he was engaged to strip cards, at half a guinea per week. He worked at this several months, living in a frugal manner, and never going into public-houses, or associating with idle company; but, when he was engaged, by the rule of the overlookers, he was forced to pay a couple of shillings, by way of footing, and then he went to a public-house in Bridge-street, where this silly and mischievous custom, let Blincoe into the first and last act of drunkenness, in which he was ever concerned, and he felt ill several days afterwards. At the same time, many of his comrades, who worked in the same room, and who contributed each so much money, got drunk also. This was spent contrary to Blincoe's wishes, who grieved that he was obliged to drink the ale. If he had refused, he would have been despised, and might have lost his employ; and if a poor fellow had been ever so low and wanted this money for the most essential purpose, it must not be refused. This is a pernicious custom, and should be abolished. Blincoe continued several months in this factory, living as it were alone in a crowd, and mixing very little with his fellow work people. From thence Blincoe went to a factory, at Bank Top, called Young's old factory, now occupied by Mr. Ramsbottom, and there, after a time, he was engaged as stoker, or engine man, doing the drudgery for the engineer. Here, he continued three years, sleeping a great part of the time on a flat stone in the fire hole. If it rained in the night he was always drenched! but he had formerly suffered so much by hardships, and the pay was so small, he determined to do his best to save as much money as might suffice to enable him to try to live as a dealer in waste cotton; from which humble state many of the most proud and prosperous of the master cotton-spinners of Manchester have emerged. His employer, liking him, raised his wages to thirteen shillings a week, and, whilst Blincoe was about as black as a chimney sweeper in full powder, the hope of future independence induced him to bear his sable hue, and his master behaved to him with more humanity, than he had been accustomed to experience. He was however disturbed by some petty artifices of the manager, in the year 1817, and an attempt being made to lower his wages, for which, upon an average, he worked sixteen hours in the day, Blincoe resolved to quit such hard, unremitting and unprofitable servitude, and from that period he commenced dealer and chapman. At the end of the first year, he found his little capital reduced full one-half; but on the other hand, he gained, in experience, more than an equivalent, to what he had lost in money, and, being pretty well initiated into the *mysteries of trade*, and having acquired a competent knowledge of raw or waste cottons, he commenced his second year, in much better style, and, at the end of that year, he had not only regained his lost capital, but added £5 to it.

Blincoe hired a warehouse and lived in lodgings. In the year 1819, on Sunday, the 27th. of June, he happened to be, with several other persons, at the christening of a neighbour's child, where several females were present. An acquaintance of Mester Blincoe's (no longer poor Blincoe,) a jolly butcher, began to jest and jeer him, as to his living single. There was a particular female friend present, whose years, though not approaching old age, outnumbered Blincoe's, and the guests ran their jokes upon her, and some of the company said, Blincoe, get married to-morrow, and then we'll have a good wedding, as well as a christening, to-day. Upon which Blincoe, leering a little sideways at the lady, said, "Well, if Martha will have me, I'll take her and marry her to-morrow." She, demurely, said "Yes." Then, said Blincoe, though taken unawares, now, if you'll stick to your word, "I will." She then said, "I'll not run from mine, if you don't." Hearing this, there was a great shout, and when it had subsided, the butcher offered to bet a leg of mutton, that Blincoe would not get married on Monday, the *28th. of June*, and others betted on the same side, when Blincoe determined to win the bets, and a wife in the bargain. Blincoe said to his comrades, "Well, that I may not be disappointed. I'll even go to see for a license to-night." Two of the party went to see all was fair. When Blincoe had got half-way, being fearful of a *hoax* by Martha, he hit on the device of holding back, telling her he could not get the license without her presence, and when she agreed to go, then still more securely to prevent his being laughed at, he said, "I have not money enough in my pocket, will you, Martha, lend me a couple of pounds?" In an instant she produced that sum, giving it to Blincoe, and they proceeded. Blincoe was so bashful he neither took her hand nor saluted her lips; but, accompanied by two of the persons who had laid wagers, went to the house direct, of the very celebrated, though not *very reverend Joshua Brookes*, lately deceased. The next morning they went in a coach from his lodgings in Bank-Top, and were married in the Old Church! Blincoe won his bets and his wife! They have lived together with as great a share of conjugal tranquillity, as falls to the lot of many, who are deemed happy couples, and he has ever since kept upon the advance in worldly prosperity. He has lived to see his tyrannical master brought to adverse fortune, to a state of comparative indigence, and, on his family, the visitation of calamities, so awful, that it looked as if the avenging power of retributive justice had laid its iron hand on him and them. In how short a time Blincoe's career will verify the prediction of the old sybil of Chapel-a-Frith remains to be seen; but it is in the compass of probability, that he may, in the meridian of his life, be carried as high, by the wheel of fortune, as the days of his infancy and youth, he was cast low!!

In the year 1824, Blincoe had accumulated in business that sum of money he thought would be sufficient to keep his family, with the exception of his cotton-waste business; shortly after he gave up a shop which he had occupied for a few years at No. 108, Bank-Top, Manchester, and took a house in Edge-place, Salford, whilst living there, thought proper to place some of the money he had saved by industry to the purchasing of some machinery for spinning of cotton—and took part of a mill of one Mr. Ormrod, near St. Paul's-Church, Tib-street, in this he was engaged six weeks, with the assistance of some mechanics, getting the machinery ready for work—the first day it was at work, an adjoining room of the building caught fire, and burnt Blincoe's machinery to the ground, not being insured, nearly ruined him.— Blincoe declares that he will have nothing to do with the spinning business again—what with the troubles endured when apprentice to it, and the heavy loss sustained by fire, is completely sick of the business altogether.

End of the Memoir of Robert Blincoe.

---

[1] Whilst Blincoe worked at Robinson's old factory, Water-street, Manchester, having, by denying himself even a sufficiency of the cheapest diet, clothed himself more respectably than he had ever been—and having two-pound notes in his pocket, he determined to spend a few shillings, and see the diversions of a horse-race, at Kersal-Moor—but not being aware that such beings as pickpockets were in the world, he put his pocket-book in his outside pocket, whence it was stolen by some of the light-fingered gentry, and poor Blincoe had to lament his want of caution.

CONFIRMATIONS OF ITS VERACITY

Ashton-under-Line, Feb. 24, 1828

DEAR SIR—I have read the narrated sufferings of Robert Blincoe with mingled sorrow and delectation: with sorrow, because I know, from bitter experience, that they have really existed; with delectation, because they have appeared before the public through the medium of the press, and may, peradventure, be the means of mitigating the misery of the unfortunate apprentices, who are serving an unexpired term of apprenticeship in various parts of Lancashire and Derbyshire. In 1806 or 7, I was bound an apprentice, with twelve others, from the workhouse of St. James, Clerkenwell London, to a Mr. J. Oxley, at Arnold-mill, near Nottingham. From thence, after two years and three months' servitude, I was sold to a Mr. Middleton, of Sheffield. The factory being burnt down at this place, I with many others, were sold to Mr. Ellice Needham, of Highgate-wall, the owner and proprietor of Litton Mill! Here I became acquainted with Robert Blincoe, better known at Litton-mill by the name of Parson. The sufferings of the apprentices were exquisite during Blincoe's servitude, both in point of hunger and acts of severity; but, subsequent to Blincoe's departure from that place, the privations we had to endure, in point of hunger, exceeded all our former sufferings (if that were possible), having to subsist principally upon woodland sustenance, or, in other words, on such food as we could extract from the woods. What I now write is to corroborate the statement of Blincoe, having heard him relate during my apprenticeship, all, or nearly all, the particulars that are now narrated in his memoir. I may also add, that I worked under Blincoe, at the same machine, in the capacity that he had done under Woodward, without receiving any harsh treatment from him—nay, so far was Blincoe from ill-treating the apprentices employed under him, that he would frequently give part of his allowance of food to those under his care, out of mere commiseration, and conceal all insignificant omissions without a word of reproach—I cannot close this letter without relating an anecdote that occurred about two years ago. Happening to call at a friend's house one day, he asked if I knew Robert Blincoe. I replied in the affirmative. Because, added he, I saw a prospectus of his biography some time past; and related the same to W. Woodward, who was on a visit here, and who immediately said, "HE'LL GIVE IT MA," and became very dejected during the remainder of his visit.

Your humble servant,

JOHN JOSEPH BETTS

Samuel Davy, a young man, now employed in the Westminster Gas Works, has called on the Publisher of BLINCOE'S MEMOIR, and has said, that his own experience is a confirmation of the general statement in the Memoir. Samuel Davy, when a child of 7 years of age, with 13 others, about the year 1805, was sent from the poorhouse of the parish of St. George's, in the Borough of

Southwark, to Mr. Watson's mill, at Penny Dam, near Preston, in Lancashire; and successively turned over to Mr. Burch's mill, at Backborough, near Castmill, and to Messrs. David and Thomas Ainsworth's mill, near Preston. The cruelty towards the children increased at each of those places, and though not quite so bad as that described by Blincoe, approached very near to it. One Richard Goodall, he describes, as entirely beaten to death! Irons were used, as with felons, in gaols, and these were often fastened on young women, in the most indecent manner from the ancles to the waist! It was common to punish the children, by keeping them nearly in a state of nudity, in the depth of winter, for several days together. Davy says, that he often thought of stealing, from the desire of getting released from such a wretched condition, by imprisonment or transportation; and, at last, at nineteen years of age, though followed by men on horseback and on foot, he successfully ran away and got to London. For ten years, this child and his brother were kept without knowing any thing of their parents, and without the parents knowing where the children were. All applications to the Parish Officers for information were vain. The supposed loss of her children, so preyed upon the mind of Davy's mother, that, with other troubles, it brought on insanity, and she died in a state of madness! No savageness in human nature, that has existed on earth, has been paralleled by that which has been associated with the English Cotton-spinning mills.

Printed in Great Britain
by Amazon

58038805R00059